RESUMES THAT GET JOBS

RESUMES THAT GET JOBS

Resume Service

Jean Reed, Editor

ARCO
New York

Fourth Edition

Copyright © 1986, 1985, 1981, 1976, 1967, 1963 by Arco Publishing, a division
of Simon & Schuster, Inc.

 ARCO

Simon & Schuster, Inc.
Gulf+Western Building
One Gulf+Western Plaza
New York, NY 10023

DISTRIBUTED BY PRENTICE HALL TRADE

Designed by Jill Schoenhaut

Manufactured in the United States of America

3 4 5 6 7 8 9 10

Library of Congress Cataloging-in-Publication Data

Résumés that get jobs.

    ''An Arco book.''
    1. Resumés (Employment) 2. Applications for
positions. I. Reed, Jean. II. Resume Service.
HF5383.G725 1986   650.1′4   86-12168
ISBN 0-668-06481-1 (Paper Edition)

CONTENTS

RESUME INDEX

Part 1

Essential Information

ABOUT RESUMES AND THE JOB SEARCH PROCESS

What Is a Resume?

Résumé is a French word meaning "summary" — pronounced REZ-*oo-may*. Although many dictionaries spell the word with accents, it is acceptable to drop them as we have in this book.

For the job applicant, a resume has become an indispensable tool. A good resume can be the most important factor in determining whether a prospective employer decides to call you in for an interview. In short, a well-prepared resume may literally get you a "foot in the door."

Additionally, an accurate, detailed resume serves another important function. It serves as a point of reference during the interview, as well as an advantageous focal point for conversation between you and the prospective employer.

How to Use Your Resume for Finding Jobs

An obvious, but limited, use of your resume is to send it where you know an opening exists. There are, however, other ways to use your resume. We suggest the following:

Seek Out Your Own Openings. If a firm, company, or organization is particularly appealing to you, send the firm your resume even though there is no apparent opening. Find out all you can about the operation in order to sound knowledgeable in your cover letter. Get an executive's name to send your resume to (use the telephone), and go to the top if necessary. Letters that are "handed down" get attention. Many good career opportunities are never advertised, and you will immediately garner points for eagerness and initiative. You have nothing to lose except your present job if you have one, so be cautious if the firm is in the same town, and stress confidentiality. It's usually respected, but be aware that there is no guarantee.

Employment Agencies. There is a big push to upgrade state agencies and the quality of job orders. Tax-paying employers are beginning to realize that they are paying for these services, and more and more are taking advantage of them. Job seekers are the benficiaries, so don't ignore these free services that are yours for the asking.

Private agencies can be expensive as well as unproductive. Ask tough questions about fees, their policy if you quit or get dismissed from any job they get you, and insist on firm, exact replies. Read what you sign, including the fine print.

Help-Wanted Advertisements. These columns are often scrutinized by employment agencies, who will call the advertiser and say, "I've got a person qualified for this job." The columns are equally available to you at no charge.

3

At certain levels they can be productive with a good resume and cover letter. If you already have a job, be cautious of blind ads. They could have been placed by your employer.

Search Firms (Headhunters). The search firm's function is to match client qualifications to job openings in a wide range of fields. Search firms don't advertise as a rule, but many will review unsolicited resumes, especially if you are in, say, upwards of a $35,000 salary bracket and have a good record of achievement. Check your local library for lists of search firms and their specialties. You may find one that matches your objective.

If you are concerned about confidentiality, write the Association of Executive Recruiting Consultants, Inc., 30 Rockefeller Plaza, Suite 914, New York, NY 10012 for their membership list. Their members agree to follow a firm policy of confidentiality.

Computer Matching. Career System is a new nationwide computer network and database information system designed to assist employers in identifying qualified professionals to fill jobs. For more information write: Career System, Corporate Service Division, 1675 Palm Beach Lakes Boulevard, West Palm Beach, Florida 33401.

RESUME FORMAT

You are cautioned at the outset to forget everything you have read or heard about resumes. While no two people agree on the exact form and content of a resume, there is, nevertheless, a sizable area of full agreement among employers and personnel people. We urge you to stay within these areas. We are, therefore, going to teach you to write the type of resume that will appeal to the people who count—those who will read the resume. The form of the resume that we shall present has been uniformly accepted by employers the nation over as concise, informative, and clear.

You will note that the first page of our resume format is a synopsis (or condensation) of the amplification that follows. This form has a distinct advantage. It enables an employer to tell at a glance whether or not he or she wants to know more about you. If an employer likes what is in the synopsis, he or she will be eager to read the amplification which follows. If the employer does not care for what is in the synopsis, you have saved everybody's time.

Following is a skeleton resume to show the basic resume form. It is practical because it is flexible. You will see that infinite variations are possible. For example, if your position is more impressive than the company name, reverse placement of "title" and "company name." However, for the sake of appearance, be consistent and follow this procedure for all employments listed. If you have an excellent education, and employment has been part-time or relatively unimportant, reverse the position of "Employment" and "Education." You will have to decide for yourself what is most important to the person who is going to read your resume.

Synopsis Part of Resume

Synopsis of Resume of: Street, City, State, Zip Code
JOHN DOE   Phone: (area code) number

<u>JOB OBJECTIVE</u>

<u>EMPLOYMENT</u>

Dates (start--end)   Name of Company, Address of Company
Present or last   Company line
  company   Job title

Dates (start--end)   Name of Company, Address of Company
                            Company line
                            Job title

Date (start--end)   Name of Company, Address of Company
                            Company line
                            Job title

<u>MISCELLANEOUS EMPLOYMENT</u>

Grouping of part-time and/or minor employments

<u>EDUCATION</u>

Dates   High School--location
  (start--finish)   Note: unnecessary if college is shown.

Dates   College name--location
  (start--finish)   Degree: Major: Minor:
                              [Class standing, _____ insert if superior]*
                              [Honors:]
                              [Expenses: percentage earned]
                              [Activities: extracurricular]
Miscellaneous   Company courses; correspondence courses;
  Education   seminars; home study.

<u>PERSONAL</u>

Age: Day, month, year of birth. [Place of birth.]
Marital Status: (married) (single) Number of children; health.
Hobbies: What you do for recreation.
Affiliations: [Optional, unless job-related.]

(FOR AMPLIFICATION SEE FOLLOWING)

*Items in brackets are optional. Later in this chapter, there is further discussion of
personal items.*

Amplified Part of Resume

Amplified Resume   John Doe
                                                                       -page 2-

EMPLOYMENT

Date of starting to present
FULL NAME OF LAST OR PRESENT COMPANY

   Responsibilities:

   Results:

   Reason for leaving:

Date of starting to date of leaving
FULL NAME OF COMPANY

   Responsibilities: (less detailed)

   Results: (less detailed)

   Reason for leaving:

Date of starting to date of leaving
FULL NAME OF COMPANY

   Responsibilities: (Note: If resume is in proper sequence,
   Results: this and ensuing employments will usual-
   Reason for leaving: ly be of less importance and correspond-
                              ingly less detailed)

MISCELLANEOUS EMPLOYMENTS
Dates can be approximate, but should indicate
frame of period involved (1975-1980)

   Group your minor (miscellaneous) employments stating in general the
   type of work. If you are under 25, group your part-time employments, particularly during school years.

   Example:
   1977-1978 Self-employed. Mowed lawns.
   1979-1980 McDonalds Restaurant. Bus boy.

References

On request

WHAT TO PUT ON YOUR RESUME

Job Objective

The Job Objective is the "soul" of your resume and should be given first and foremost consideration. Job Objective says what you want to do and it should say it as clearly and concisely as possible.

Decide the type of a job for which you are best equipped by reason of your temperament, personal preferences, capabilities, and experience—then state it. If it is in sales, what kind? Is management your goal? Any travel restrictions? This would then be stated, "Position in tangible sales leading to management. Prefer limited travel." Note examples on the actual resumes in this book. Unless you have strong geographical preferences, do not state them. It serves only to narrow the scope of your availability.

Suppose you do not have very definite or well-defined objectives; or perhaps you have several. You may consider comprehensive job counseling, or at least discuss your background with an employment counselor to determine the best statement of your objectives. In any event, we urge you to avoid the "all-purpose— will do anything" type of objective. You cannot sell a product successfully unless you are specific about its advantages to the buyer.

Employment

List employment in reverse chronological order (your present or last job *first*, etc.). Be certain you list starting and leaving dates, your position title, exact name of company and present address. If the company has changed name or address since you were there, state "Jones-Smith Co., 114 Main St., Newark, NJ (formerly known as Smith Co., 90 South Ave., Camden, NJ)." Company line is for purposes of identification only and is not necessary when it is well known nationally, or if identification is obvious from the company name. Example: "Morris *Lumber* Company."

To state salary is to lose your bargaining power. At the interview, your salary will, and *must*, be discussed. However, for resume purposes, showing the percentage of increase (if noteworthy) in the amplification portion is a safe middle road to travel. At the executive level, we suggest "salary in low, medium, or high five figures" as a method of establishing your level without pinpointing the exact amount. This can appear in one line of the synopsis page.

Education

The further you are away from school, the less educational detail is required. Use the form shown on page 5 to set forth your education clearly and concisely—fitting it, of course, to your particular situation. Make certain that the name and location of schools are correct, as well as the dates attended, especially if your education shows a continued effort at self-improvement, as indicated by fairly recent courses.

Recent graduates have little but education for sale. Therefore they should cover this area thoroughly, listing not only their majors and minors, but any and all subjects related to their fields of interest. We also suggest listing semester hours and grades when better than average. Extracurricular activities are important, for they indicate a well-rounded personality and demonstrate social awareness. This importance, of course, diminishes with time—so again, the older you are, and further away from school, the fewer items you should list.

Work during college for the recent graduate can be shown on the synopsis page under "Employment," and/or on page 6 (the Amplification part of your resume) as space permits.

Do *not* omit your education because it is limited. Enlarge upon it where possible by listing company courses, home-study courses, etc. This indicates a desire for self-education readily understood by the often sympathetic employer, who (like you) may not have had the opportunity for extensive formal education. The same employer will not be equally sympathetic to amateurish attempts at bluffing an education you do not have.

Personal Data

There is no pat answer to the frequently asked (and argued) question: How much personal information should be in a resume?

It is illegal in some states to attach a photograph, and there are enough conflicting rules and regulations to give both employer and job applicant a raging headache over what can and cannot be asked.

However, there is no law that says you cannot volunteer positive, personal information that will give you a cutting edge.

The employer is hiring you, the individual, as well as your set of qualifications; consequently, isn't it common sense to paint your best possible word picture?

If you're under age thirty-five, stating your age in this youth-oriented society only makes good sense. If you're over, give year of birth or say "mature." Or say nothing. It's your picture; choose your own colors.

As to marital status, if you're not married, you're single. Your divorce record is your business. Dependent children under your roof are really nobody's business, but again, they might serve to enhance your "good family person" picture.

Health is always good or excellent, unless you have some specific impairment that places some limitations on job performance. Handle it by keeping it off your resume altogether. This can be covered at the interview.

Owning your own home tends to suggest "roots" and "stability," and if this is the image you want to project, go right ahead.

Hobbies flesh out your portrait, so by all means include them. A word of warning: Do not give yourself a fanciful hobby in an attempt to impress. A good interviewer will nail you for it, and it's a dumb way to blow a good career opportunity.

Affiliations, particularly when job-related, can serve to put the finishing touches to your word picture. Community involvement as indicated by participation in Rotary, United Way, Shriners, etc., is positive input.

Consequently, to put to final rest the question of how much personal information to volunteer in a resume, the answer is: write anything that is positive and improves your image.

Military Service

If service is recent and extensive, it can be on the synopsis page and amplified. Otherwise, a lone line regarding it, under "personal," will serve.

The recently discharged serviceman or -woman (like the recent graduate) has little but service experience, education, and training to sell, and should give these emphasis. Generally speaking, select the functions you performed most capably and relate them to a civilian occupation field.

Analysis of Amplification Preparation

Before we discuss writing up the details of your history, let us review briefly just what a resume is. A resume, in essence, is a piece of direct mail advertising—*and the product is YOU.*

Effective direct mail advertising is: (1) attractive in appearance; (2) provocative in content; (3) positive in approach. Emphasis is *always* on what the product has done and is capable of doing, *never* on what it has not done and why. Keep this foremost in your mind when you are preparing your own "direct mail advertising."

As we have said previously, the sole purpose of a resume is to arouse interest and to get you an interview. Save some ammunition for that interview, but get enough into the resume to make the interviewer want to know more about you—to call you in and talk with you. Strive to sound like a good investment.

Responsibilities

State in what capacity you were employed and what you were expected to do. Also state level of responsibility. Use phrases like "completely responsible for," etc. Many jobs involve familiarity with certain kinds of equipment or processes. For instance, in data processing: state any equipment within your experience, and what you are able to do with it—operate, program; in purchasing: state type of materials, components, etc., you have purchased; in manufacturing: state kinds of equipment involved.*

Results

This is the body of your resume, for here you set yourself apart from the "herd" through accomplishment. Everyone has responsibilities, but not everyone fulfills them to the same degree. Results give you stature above and beyond a formal (sometimes meaningless) title bestowed on you by a firm. Again, remember the advertising approach. Point up what you can do by showing what you have done. You must sell your value to a company as deftly and effectively as it sells its products to the public. For example, if you are a salesperson, alert the employer to the fact that you are a good one by the simple expedient of showing increased sales volume. Perhaps you only maintained sales volume but you did so under unusual difficulties. State what they were, and how you overcame them.

In many fields, results cannot be measured in so simple a fashion. However, salary increase is a "result," promotion is a "result," increased responsibilities can be a "result." You might have received recognition in the form of an award or completed a project outside the framework of your responsibilities and received no particular recognition for it. Reward yourself in your resume by stating what you did. If necessary, list such extracurricular activity under a heading "Special Accomplishments."

If you have been with one firm a long time it is sometimes difficult to show concrete results. Employ the "progression" technique. The principle involved here is simple. To have started as a delivery boy and to have ended up as a file clerk makes you a more important file clerk.

Miscellaneous or Part-Time Work Details

State what you did in general terms (selling, construction, general office work) but where possible state name of company. This gives credence to your statements. Also make certain you give the approximate dates this miscellaneous work period covered. The purpose of this grouping is twofold: (1) it shortens your resume and yet still accounts for all your working years; (2) it avoids the impression of job-hopping.

Reason for Leaving

Ordinarily the reason for leaving should be given for each employment to which you give an individual listing. Don't get involved or verbose. A simple "for a better job" or "to improve status" will often do it.

If your most recent job represents your highest skills (as it probably does), we suggest that you give it most space. If it has resulted from a definite progression from earlier jobs, such jobs can be covered more briefly.

On the other hand, at times the reason for leaving cannot be stated tersely because actually it came about through a complex situation involving other people, kind of work, rate of pay, and other factors. Try to tell your story clearly and concisely avoiding phrases which reflect unfavorably upon you. For example, "No chance for advancement." (Why did you take the job in the first place?) Try "Arrived at dead end." instead.

If your reason for leaving is a battle with your boss, "Disagreement with management policies." sounds less peevish than "Disagreement with management." If your salary check remained the same for too long, "Salary did not keep pace with increased productivity." says more for you than "No salary increase."

Eventually, an employer will probably want to cover these matters thoroughly, but for resume purposes brevity without bitterness is the rule. If all else fails, use the entirely safe and acceptable reason for leaving "will be discussed at interview."

Length of Resume

We do not deem it advisable to make arbitrary statements on resume length. Length will vary to the same degree that individual records vary. However, we have found the average record can be handled satisfactorily in two pages (counting synopsis sheet as one).

Occasionally a complex or highly varied record requires a third page to tell the story properly and to avoid overcrowding. If employers like what they see at a glance, their appetite is whetted for detail; therefore, they proceed with an eye to content rather than page number. For practical purposes, a good rule of thumb is two-page minimum, three-page maximum.

Person and Tense

The rule is not rigid. However, consider these phrasings:

1. "As a result of my efficient discharge of duties, I was promoted."
2. "As a result of his efficient discharge of duties, he was promoted."
3. "As a result of efficient discharge of duties, was promoted."

We believe the last phrasing is the most pleasing to read; it also makes the strongest statement. Many self-prepared resumes make the mistake of being too modest. Deleting the first person "I" may make it easier for you to give yourself proper credit without feeling boastful.

References

Unless references are requested, most employers are unimpressed by such a list. There are two good reasons for this: (1) Any name you list is obviously a "friend," understandably prejudiced in your favor; (2) the word of a past employer is not necessarily significant. Prospective employers are aware that it is not an uncommon practice for a past employer to give a likeable yet unsatisfactory worker a "break" in the form of a good reference. These and other factors serve to render the reference list of little or no value. For resume purposes, stating "References Available" is a safe, standard, and acceptable practice.

You may disagree. If so, there is no harm in listing your references. We simply believe it does little good in the resume itself.

Physical Preparation of Resume

Just as you are not inclined to buy a product in a soiled wrapper, an employer does not "buy" you on cheap paper, messy with erasures and misspelled words. A resume *must* be typed. A well-typed resume is always acceptable (never a carbon). Your alternative is to have your resume duplicated by a professional business service (check the Yellow Pages, usually under "Photocopy"). Type, or have typed, your initial copy following our basic format. If you have it typed, you need not be concerned about spacing, placing, etc., for any reputable firm which specializes in typing resumes can, and will, set it up attractively. The cost of duplication on good bond of 50 to 100 copies of a two- to three-page resume usually will not exceed pennies per page—and since your position may hinge upon it, it is money well spent.

Resist all suggestions or advice to use a marker pen on your resume for "emphasis." Proper emphasis is achieved in a resume by clear format and consise, meaty content. Colored underscoring and marginal notes are childish.

Do not use a resume cover. A few die-hards still persist in encasing their typed resume in expensive cardboard or vinyl covers. Don't be one of them. It's the mark of an amateur, a showoff, or both. More important, however, covers irritate prospective employers. They don't fit in their resume files. They do fit in their round one.

ANSWERING CLASSIFIED ADS

"Wanted: mature, responsible, full-time salesperson."

It is assumed that you have armed yourself with a good resume before answering a classified advertisement.

The next step is writing a specific cover letter. Specific ad-answering technique does not vary appreciably from the technique of writing any good covering letter of application, except for one point. Follow the advertisement line so that you will sound tailor-made for the job. See the following cover letter, which is slanted to the above advertisement.

Dear Sir:

In response to your advertisement in the August 10th issue of the *Daily Chronicle*, I am a mature woman in good health, and I should like to apply for the position in sales with your organization.

I have had previous department store experience, own my own home and car, and am free to accept a full-time position. I have no objection to overtime or weekend work if required.

My employment background as well as my phone number are on the attached resume. Thank you for reviewing it, and I shall look forward to hearing from you.

Sincerely,

Eleanor Adison

GENERAL COVER LETTERS

Always enclose a cover letter when you mail out a resume.

Cover letters should be individually typed and signed. Anything else indicates a serious lack of interest, and a lack of elementary business courtesy as well.

Your cover letter should be brief and follow these general guidelines:

1. Address your letter to a specific person. Employers are people, and people tend to be complimented when you know their names and titles. Consequently, it's worthwhile to make an effort to find them out.

   If the company you are applying to is located nearby, phone and ask for the name of the president, or sales manager, or personnel manager, etc. It's not necessary to identify yourself or your reason for calling. If you should be pressed, a disarming "I want to write him (her) a letter" will usually do the trick.

   If the job is important enough, this call should be made wherever the company is located. Don't rely on some friend's recollection of a name or on personnel records. These records get out of date rapidly, and a letter addressed to a predecessor immediately labels you as a person with a certain carelessness for meaningful detail.

2. Your letter need not cover the same ground as your resume. It should merely sum up what you have to offer and act as an introduction for your resume.

3. Let your letter reflect your individuality, but avoid appearing familiar, overbearing, humorous, or cute.

4. With local firms, take the initiative in suggesting that you telephone for an interview.

5. With out-of-town or-state firms, it is imperative that you indicate willingness to make the trip for a personal interview. Better yet, give dates when you could be in the area for an interview.

Sample Cover Letter

1877 Orange Ave.
Sarasota, Florida 33579

Mr. George Howe, Manager
Howe Realtors
29 Prospect St.
Sarasota, Florida 33581

Dear Mr. Howe:

I want to be a real estate salesperson with the Howe corporation.

With my recently acquired Florida Real Estate License, I know that working for your highly respected company would be the ideal way for me to learn the practical sales skills needed to supplement enthusiasm and education.

At present, I realize that my most useful skills may be typing and knowledge of general office procedures. However, I have no inflated aspirations of starting at the top. I expect to reach it, but first I am anxious to learn and for an opportunity to demonstrate my ability.

My resume is enclosed for your review. May I call your secretary for an interview appointment?
Thank you.

Sincerely

(Signed: Lois Gunther)

Lois Gunther

enc: resume

(A generally good approach when sending out a resume "cold," i.e., without any knowledge that an opening may exist. Requires a bit more "self-sell" to generate interest in getting resume read.)

Synopsis of Resume of: 1877 Orange Ave.
LOIS GUNTHER   Sarasota, FL 33579
                                          Phone: (803) 922-0778

JOB OBJECTIVE

Real Estate Salesperson

EDUCATION

1982   Principles and Practices of Real Estate
                    St. Loo's College (extension)

Other: Real Estate License Law Course
                    Reagon Specialized School of Instruction

License: Florida Real Estate Salesperson's License
                    Received November, 1980
                Notary-Public-at-large, State of Florida
                    Commission valid through 1984

College: University of Florida
                    B.A. in History

EXPERIENCE

10/81-Pres.   Boomhower Real Estate Company
                Arcadia, FL.

10/80-10/81   Lindsey Title and Mortgage
                Miami, FL

1978-1980   Lee County Schools, Ft. Myers, FL
                History teacher

Other: General office work, sales

PERSONAL

Born: 1956. Single parent of one school-age child. Health:
                excellent.
Finances: Own car, home, income property.
Hobbies: Sports car rallying; sewing; reading.
Affiliations: Sarasota Board of Realtors
                Florida Board of Realtors
                National Board of Realtors

(FOR AMPLIFICATION SEE FOLLOWING)

*(Note: Ms. Gunther is changing fields; consequently her former profession is
deemphasized in favor of her newly acquired education in her present field, plus a
focus on the sales aspects of her former record — a needed tool in the new field.)*

Amplified Resume   Lois Gunther
                                                                   -page 2-

EMPLOYMENT HIGHLIGHTS

October 1981-Present
BOOMHOWER REALTORS
    Accepted position as salesperson with assurance that would enter
planned sales training program under guidance of an experienced
member of the sales force.

    Program failed to materialize; would make change to company that
would provide background training in the practical aspects of
selling to complement and embellish theories and principles
learned in acquiring recent real estate license.

10/80-10/81
LINDSEY TITLE AND MORTGAGE
    Accepted position as mortgage clerk to obtain practical experience
in real estate field. Responsible for shipping out recorded closing instruments and typing of title insurance policies.

    Was given occasional opportunities to go into field for sales in-
doctrination and found this to be best area and ultimate goal.

    Reason for leaving: To accept sales training leading to full-
time sales position with major firm above.

1978-1980
LEE COUNTY SCHOOLS
    Taught History at junior high level; also responsible for school
library.

    During summer of 1979, was offered position as manager of the
Taylor Galleries in Ft. Myers. Encompassed myriad responsibilities including sales promotion of rare paintings, sculpture, and
sundry objets d'art. Customers ranged from general tourists
to visiting dignataries.

    Handled all books, all relevant correspondence; closed sales.
Offered year-round position following; was unable to accept.

REFERENCES

In confidence, on request

HOW EMPLOYERS READ RESUMES

By Thomas McElheny, Ph. D., founder and president of the American Center for Management and Professional Development, which employs approximately 125 personnel. The company sets up and conducts nationwide management development seminars for major Fortune 500 companies.

The first thing I look for in a resume is problem-solving ability—the ability to create solutions as opposed to creating problems. I am not so concerned that someone has worked at a place for seven or eight years. At the same time, I don't want to see a pattern of change every six months. There has to be a reasonable in-between.

I look at the positions held. For example, "shipping clerk." That title is not descriptive in and of itself. Our shipping clerk is a person who has to think on his feet, solve problems, and make decisions. Another shipping clerk may be someone who carries boxes from point *A* to point *B*. Consequently, I don't accept just the job title. I want to see the work detailed in the resume.

I look for character. Integrity and commitment are important to me. A tip-off of lack of commitment would be excessive changing of jobs. If the change is obviously to improve status, yes. But if a person has been trained by a company and quit on a whim, that's cheating.

I am turned off by incomplete information. When I read "college degree" or "B.S.," I want to know what school, what year, what was your major. At the same time, don't kill me with details such as "President of the Drama Club."

I like enough personal information to get an accurate visual picture. For example, a former officer in the armed services would mean to me presence, assertiveness, and leadership qualities. I highly endorse hobbies and ask about them to make sure they are not there just to impress me.

I am offended when I feel the resume is written in an attempt to manipulate me. Don't try to hide your age from me. If you've had twenty-five years of hands-on experience, it tells me you're no kid, but in a positive way.

On the other hand, if an applicant takes the time to find out about my organization, our needs and requirements, and sends me a resume slanted to that extent, I am not offended. I am flattered.

We hire speakers, and I receive perhaps twenty-five resumes a week [for these jobs]. The first thing I do is turn everybody down four times. If they don't have the innate persistence to do whatever it takes to get to me, I'm not interested.

Secondly, I look at the personality of the applicant to see if it matches my needs. To be a speaker you have to have academic credentials, but there is a way to say you're an expert without being an ass.

The key characteristic for a platform speaker is to be able to keep an adult audience interested in your topic for eight hours a day for three days on end. It requires a high energy, interest, and knowledge level. I look for that.

When I get a package of eighty-two pages of articles an applicant wrote, it tells me that he or she doesn't know very much about this business.

The distinctive resume that jumps out at me is the resume that pinpoints a candidate's ability to give a good presentation. I don't care if they are 110 pounds or 300 pounds if they can utilize their image to give a good presentation. One of my best speakers is not very attractive physically, but he's a huggy teddy bear. He's taken his physical attributes and maximized the impact.

His resume was to the point and the references he listed were well-known, good people in the field. Normally, references do not impress me at all, especially on the standard job resume. The only form I find acceptable is "On Request."

Prior salary levels do not turn me off at all. If someone is honest enough to tell me what he or she made, there are trade-offs. I may be paying less with more opportunity. Nevertheless, I think I'd leave salary off a job resume. A resume is a selling tool, and in selling, the idea is to create interest but not to give so much information you kill the sale.

I like affiliations too. I like the fact that an applicant is involved with the United Way and various community organizations. The evidence is that there is something in life more important than their own concerns.

People whose focus is entirely on themselves eventually are going to crash.

INTERVIEW STRATEGY

Questions You Can Be Asked During the Interview

Name and Address. You must give your name and address, and can be asked how long you've resided at that address, or in your employer's city and state. You can be asked whether you have worked for that company under a different name, changed your name, or ever used an assumed name so that the employer can check your previous work record.

Work Experience. You can be asked for names and addresses of previous employers, your duties there and the length of time you held the job, your promotions, and your reasons for leaving.

Education. You can be asked about your educational background in detail.

Convictions for Crime. You can be asked whether you have ever been convicted of a crime and for the details. You cannot be asked about arrests—only convictions.

Questions You Should Not Be Asked During an Interview

The law says when you apply for a job you cannot be discriminated against because of your race, color, national origin, religion, sex, age, and in some cases, physical or mental handicaps.

This sounds straightforward, but unfortunately it isn't always so clear. However, employers and applicants must carry on, trying to live within both the federal laws and the state antibias laws, and the following guidelines have been developed as to how sensitive topics should be handled to avoid conflict with federal and state laws.

Race or Color. Neither should be the subject of any comment in an interview, and you should not be asked for a picture of yourself when you apply for a job.

National Origin. You should not be asked about your national origin, lineage, ancestry, or descent, or that of your spouse, unless the employer is an organization promoting a particular national heritage.

Religion. You should not be asked about your religious background or beliefs. Your religious convictions could be relevant to a job (a workweek that might violate your religious ethic, for example). But the employer cannot raise the issue by asking about your religion or by suggesting that you might object to the job for that reason.

Sex and Marital Status. Beyond clear-cut examples such as a lingerie clerk or a commercial actor, sex should not enter into the hiring interview discussion. You should not be asked about your marital status, whether your spouse works, or even who you would like notified in case of an emergency. Questions about children, child-care arrangements, likelihood of pregnancy, and your views on birth control are similarly no-nos.

Age. As long as you are an adult under seventy years of age, your age should be irrelevant, unless age enters into the specific function of the job. For example, let's say the job is that of a smoke jumper who jumps out of airplanes to fight forest fires. There has been reasonable medical evidence that anyone over forty cannot do it without an extraordinary increase in risk. In this case the employer can discriminate against anyone over forty, because he is discriminating against everyone over forty, not just you. Airlines were not successful in establishing that persons over a certain age were not able to fulfill flight attendant functions; consequently, their hard-and-fast age rule went by the board.

Handicaps. Federal laws prohibit U.S. government agencies and contractors from discrimination in hiring on the basis of physical or mental handicaps. Some states have similar laws. Once an employer has detailed the requirements of a job, you could be asked whether you have any physical or mental problems that would preclude your satisfactorily performing the job.

Commonly Asked Interview Questions and How to Answer Them

1. *Tell me something about yourself.*

   Know your resume details and state them concisely.

2. *Why do you want to work for us?*

   Do whatever research possible ahead of time to be ready for this question. Explain that you are impressed with their policies, reputation, working conditions, physical plant—whatever seems germane.

3. *Why should I hire you?*

   Because you are uniquely qualified and your personal goals coincide with theirs. Explain what you can bring to the job.

4. *Why did you leave your last job?*

   Tell it like your resume says.

5. *Why are you thinking of leaving your present job?*

   Be honest, be brief, but be prepared. Internal politics, dead end, too much pressure, too little salary are all acceptable, understandable reasons.

6. *What are your strengths?*

   Careful study of your resume in advance will prepare you for this question, plus help you document your reply. Does it reveal leadership? Ambition? Loyalty? Determination? Ability to work under pressure? To cope? To get along with people? Steady work record? Extraordinary abilities (sales, administrative)?

7. *What are your weaknesses?*

   Nobody's perfect, but be easy on yourself. Don't be negative. You can turn this to your advantage by thinking it through ahead of time. For example, "I have a temper—but one of my strengths is that I have learned to control it."

8. *Where do you expect to be ten or twenty years from now?*

   This is a favorite. Think it through carefully and resist all temptations to make a flip response. "In your job" can be a dangerous reply to an insecure man or woman. Expecting promotions and salary increases commensurate with your productiveness is good.

9. *What is the minimum salary you would find acceptable?*

Know the salary range of the job and inquire if this is in line with their scale. Stress job satisfaction and willingness to accept a starting figure you can genuinely live with. Negotiate if necessary.

10. *When could you start work here?*

If not working—immediately! If working, play fair with your present employer—a week to two weeks notice if in a non-supervisory capacity; one month minimum in management or supervisory capacity.

Questions You Should Ask a Prospective Employer

1. What would my duties and responsiblities be? Or, if it is a large firm, they may have a prepared job description. Ask for it.
2. If salary has not yet been discussed, broach it in the same manner discussed under interviewer questions.
3. For whom will I be working for and with? What will my hours be?
4. What are my opportunities for advancement? Raises?
5. What are my opportunities for additional training and/or education?
6. What are your employee benefits?
7. What are your (company/firm/store) policies on: holidays, lunch, dress, smoking, coffee breaks?
8. Are employees paid every week—every two weeks?
9. Is there any additional information with which I can provide you to aid your evaluation of me for this position?
10. May I ask when I can expect a decision regarding this position?

AFTER THE INTERVIEW COURTESY

According to corporate personnel directors, only one percent of job applicants follow up an interview with a letter of thanks. Often they are among the chosen few who get job offers, because this simple, courteous gesture makes them stand out from the rest.

The smart job applicant will send a brief thank-you letter the same day as the interview or, at the latest, the day after the interview.

This letter may be handwritten if your handwriting is legible, or typed if you own a typewriter. If the answer is "negative" to both, enlist the aid of a friend or business service. See the following letter for an example.

Date

Mr. John Interviewer, Personnel Manager
Smith and Wesson Company
88 State St.
Podunk, NY 19120

Dear Mr. Interviewer:

I want to express my thanks to you for the time and courtesy extended
to me today. I enjoyed the conversation with you, and am even more en-
thusiastic about the position you have to offer after hearing more about
your company and the exciting career opportunities.

I believe my experience and skills would permit me to make some valuable contributions to your fine firm for our mutual benefit.

I will call you in a few days and hope you will have reached a decision
favorable to me.

Sincerely,

THE INTERVIEW FROM THE EMPLOYER'S VIEWPOINT

This is the philosophy and strategy used in screening resumes and conducting employment interviews by Vincent M. Tarduogno, Assistant Vice-President and Administrative Manager of Merrill, Lynch, Pierce, Fenner & Smith. Mr. Tarduogno also conducts "Employee Selection and Hiring Practices" seminars and workshops at the University of South Florida; he holds an M.B.A. from Michigan State University.

Initial employment screening is, of course, done through resumes. I expect a resume to be clean, easy to read, and on quality paper. I like the content to flow and to give me an overview of the person, starting with his or her most recent experience and working backward.

I like some verbiage on what has been accomplished within a particular job, and I look for consistency in job change, and that there are no lapses in time. I look for stability. For example, are there a lot of restless jumps in jobs, or do the applicants move from job to job in a logical fashion? What kinds of choices have they made in their life? Why have they made these choices? Is the new job significantly better?

I like enough personal information to get a verbal snapshot. In short, lay out a clear picture of yourself, but don't volunteer negative information. Education should be included, but if you have less than a three-point-zero grade average in college, don't bother putting it in a resume. But don't lie. Most good interviewers have a sixth sense, and they'll catch you at it.

The biggest turnoff to me is not being able to follow chronologically on a resume, and using the functional approach such as "selling skills," "managerial skills." This is too involved for a resume. That's for me to find out on the interview. All I'm looking for is to have my appetite whetted as to whether I have an interest in pursuing this person further.

As to the actual interview, I think the question "Tell me about yourself" is a bad interview question. It is a stress-inducing question and the job of a good interviewer is to put the candidate at ease.

Nonetheless, if someone asks you that stressful question, you almost have to answer it, so be prepared. Make notes and rehearse at home so that under stress you won't blurt out some negative information in a nervous compulsion to fill the silence.

On an initial interview, I ask why applicants want to make a change and why they think they would like to work for us. This way I find out if they have a reasonable concept of the job they are applying for and why they want to make a change. I ask them what contributions they made to their organization, things they are most proud of. Then I ask about their frustrations and disappointments.

I ask if they have any questions to ask of me. This gives me further indication of their interest and how well the candidates have done their homework.

When I am interviewing a stockbroker candidate, for instance, I will look for sales orientation. Demeanor and physical appearance are important because a stockbroker will have to deal with the public on an ongoing basis. If a candidate has a sloppy appearance, he or she had better offer some other qualities which overwhelm me during that first meeting. It's also important that a candidate not slaughter the King's English.

In the initial conversation, one thing I try to find out is if a candidate will really fit into this corporate environment. For example, if you find a person who likes structure and black-and-white answers, he will not like it here. Nor will a person who likes a nice peaceful, quiet environment. These things give me a reasonably quick indication that it will not be a good match.

At our firm we train our own people after they are hired at a cost of several thousand dollars, which points out why short-term employments are red flags.

After a person is trained and proved productive, someone outside is always willing to pay more. Another employer will get a trained employee he didn't have to pay to train, so he can, therefore, offer a higher salary.

The benefit to the employee is a quick buck, but there are a lot of intangibles he loses out on. This is where people have to assess painstakingly what they are looking for in their careers and the choices they make.

An astute interviewer will not accept "The job wasn't all it was cracked up to be" as a viable excuse more than once. What the interviewer sees is that you did not take time to investigate the job thoroughly before you jumped at the money bait. This denotes poor decision-making, especially when there is a pattern of this type of activity.

Job candidates at our firm go through several tests and interviews before the final interview, which can run two to three hours.

I tell college students, if you have an employer who says, "You're hired" after a half-hour interview, be wary. Even in a fast-food world, do not accept fast job offers without question. Insist on getting your questions answered. Or at least know what you're getting yourself into. If it's a sink-or-swim situation, know it in advance.

I don't like game-playing in the hiring process. If I like your resume and call you in for an interview, it's a two-way street. We are both doing a selling job on one another in a sense, and we owe one another mutual respect and courtesy.

You are not a second-class citizen because you want to change a job, want a better job, or happen to be out of a job. I want people who are as interested in learning about the career opportunities we have to offer as I am to learn about what they have to offer.

[Hiring] is like creating a good marriage. It involves the melding of minds. You have to know that what I have to offer is going to match your needs, and vice versa.

If each of us takes the time to find out everything we need to know, we'll make a better decision. And the chances of sticking with that commitment are going to be much greater.

SOCIAL SECURITY

Your Earnings Record

Your employer is required to give you a form showing the amount of your earnings that counts for social security. He does this at the end of the year (or when you stop working for him if it is before the end of the year). These receipts (usually a W-2 form "Wage and Tax Statement") will help you should there be an error in the amount of earnings reported on the social security record.

The social security administration has a special lifetime earnings record for you at its headquarters in Baltimore, Maryland. This record is available to you at any time, and will be sent at no charge merely by filling out the card shown on the following page (available at your social security office for the asking).

It is prudent to request this every three years or so, to make certain the social security taxes you are paying are being properly credited to your social security account. If there is an error, the more recently it was made the easier it is to correct. In some instances, after approximately three years have passed an error cannot be corrected; the record stands.

REQUEST FOR STATEMENT OF EARNINGS

SOCIAL SECURITY NUMBER →

DATE OF BIRTH →

MONTH	DAY	YEAR

Please send a statement of my Social Security earnings to:

NAME { MISS MRS. MR. } _____

STREET & NUMBER _____

CITY & STATE _____ ZIP CODE _____

Print Name and Address in Ink Or Use Typewriter

SIGN YOUR NAME HERE (DO NOT PRINT) _____

Sign your own name only. Under the law, information in your social security record is confidential and anyone who signs another person's name can be prosecuted.

If you have changed your name from that shown on your social security card, please copy your name below exactly as it appears on your card.

Part 2

Sample Resumes

HOW TO USE THE SAMPLE RESUMES

The sample resumes cover practically every employment category and job application, and were prepared by a professional resume firm which keeps abreast of employment trends and practices. The form, theory, and philosophy in these resumes represent employer thinking nationwide. The resume format offered is accepted as the standard, approved format for clarity of presentation and effectiveness of design.

If you cannot find the exact position for which you are applying, refer to the resume index at the front of the book. Look for the job titles that are closest. After locating the model that most closely parallels your own situation, use it as a model to structure your own resume.

Read all the resumes that in some way relate to your particular background or job objective. This will enable you to pick and choose valuable ideas that may be neatly incorporated into your own resume.

Note the editor's comments at the bottom of some resumes. They show how various problem areas are treated, and can help your resume preparation should your career background not fit into any standard mold.

Synopsis of Resume of:
STEWART T. MORRIS

62 Crestview Park
Rogers City, MI 49779
Phone: (517) 813-8903

JOB OBJECTIVE

Educational Administration

EMPLOYMENT

1981-Present   SUPERINTENDENT OF SCHOOLS
Rogers City, MI

1967-1981   SUPERVISING PRINCIPAL
Board of Education, Cheboygan, MI

1969-1979   DIRECTOR PHYSICAL EDUCATION
Board of Education, Gaylord, MI

EDUCATION

1964-1968   State University of Michigan, Ann Arbor, MI
(Completed five-year course in four years)
Degrees: B.S. in Physical Education.
           A.B. (cum laude) - Science minor
           M.S. in Education (1977)
Activities: Varsity basketball; all intramural sports;
received cup for all-around athletic
achievement; social fraternity - president
senior year.
Note: Total of 20 hours beyond Master's Degree,
acquired as time and location have permitted.
Expects to continue on same basis.

PERSONAL

Born: 6/5/44. Married. Two teenage children. Health: excellent.

Residence: Owns home and summer cottage; willing to relocate.

Hobbies: Sports (active and spectator); music appreciation.

Affiliations: Rotary International; Michigan State Teachers Association; Michigan State City and Village Superintendents; active in local affairs -- see following for complete listing.

(FOR AMPLIFICATION SEE FOLLOWING)

Stressing success in handling people, as well as esteem in which applicant is held as indicated by elective office and membership in responsible organizations; personal statements show good family man, stability; record merits three pages.

Amplified Resume   Stewart T. Morris
                                                    -page 2-

EMPLOYMENT HIGHLIGHTS

1981-Present
SUPERINTENDENT OF SCHOOLS
   Employed as Superintendent of system composed of a Senior High,
   Junion High, and four elementary schools.

   Directed school system centralization with outlying districts. Bus
   routes have been put into operation; approximately $12,000,000 in
   new buildings have been added (three complete buildings plus other
   additions); four bond issues have been proposed to and passed by
   the community.

   Faculty has grown from 85 to 120; student body has increased from
   1,500 to 2,700. Scholarship has been maintained at a high level.
   Pupil achievement averages are in top percentile of country;
   scholarships earned by students in system have risen to 16 of the
   25 offered to all systems in county. Employee turnover remarkably
   low - losses to other systems almost nil. In public relations area
   has successfully accomplished difficult task of pleasing public,
   faculty, and students during a period of constant change and multi-
   tudinous school money problems.

   Responsibilities include: (1) Preparation, presentation, and enforcement of budgets. (2) Finding and hiring qualified teachers.
   (3) Curriculum planning and equipment procurement. (4) Overall
   supervision of all schools in system. (5) Contact with and follow-
   up on architectural planning and construction of all buildings,
   plus specifying and installing all new equipment. (6) Personnel
   Supervisor.

   Reason for desiring change: Desires to leave public life.

1979-1981
SUPERVISING PRINCIPAL
   As Supervising Principal was confronted with task of taking school
   through complex centralization procedures.

   Spoke to groups of citizens at all levels; successfully solved the
   multiple problems which arose. Supervised planning and construction
   of new centralized building, as well as its ultimate operation and
   operating personnel.

   Reason for leaving: To accept position above.

(continued)

Amplified Resume   Stewart T. Morris
                                                       -page 3-

1969-1979
DIRECTOR PHYSICAL EDUCATION
    Coached all athletic teams; planned all gymnasium programs. Success
    indicated by record of winning teams (several championships in bas-
    ketball and football) in addition to outstanding record of coopera-
    tion from both students and other faculty members. Completed
    Masters in Education during this period; left to take supervisory
    position.

GENERAL

Activities include:

1. President of Central Zone of Michigan State Teachers' Associa-
    tion (10,000 teachers).

2. State Director, Michigan State Teachers' Association.

3. Chairman Michigan State Fund Raising Drive for Retired Teachers'
    Home.

4. Past Chairman Michigan State Teachers' Public Relations Committee.

5. Past President Rogers City Rotary Club.

6. Board of Directors of: Rogers City Savings Bank, Michigan State
    Public High School Athletic Association, Michigan State Public
    High School Athletic Protection Plan (insurance).

7. Chairman: Christmas and Easter Seal Drive, annual Red Cross
    Drive, Civic Music Association Drive.

8. Member Executive Committee Michigan State High School Athletic
    Association.

REFERENCES

Available

Synopsis of Resume of:
CLINTON L. SEYMOUR

300 Rosemoor Dr.
Chicago, IL 60648
Phone: (312) 497-8745

JOB OBJECTIVE

Position in field of Industrial Relations, utilizing personnel,
science, industrial, engineering, and accounting background

EMPLOYMENT

1980-Present   PERSONNEL DIRECTOR
Photo Products Division (present position)
Progressed through Tabulating Research, Industrial
Engineering, and Inventory Control positions.
Apex Camera Co., Chicago, IL

1978-1980   Management Trainee. Two-year program.
Left on completion; wished to change fields.
United Life Insurance Co., New York, NY

1975-1978   General Office Work. Offered managerial training.
During and after college period; resigned to accept
position above.
Harrison Electric Products Co., Louisville, KY

EDUCATION

1971-1975   University of Louisville, Louisville, KY
Degrees: B.S. in Business Administration
           B.S. in Chemistry
Honors: Offered fellowship for graduate study;
          finances prevented acceptance.

Current   Company courses in:
Industrial Engineering, MTM (Methods, Time, Measure-
ment), Conference Leadership, Human Relations, Work
Measurement.

PERSONAL

Born: 6/30/51, married, good health.
Residence: Owns home; will relocate for proper opportunity.
Hobbies: Sailing; golf; bridge.
Affiliations: Industrial Management Council.

(FOR AMPLIFICATION SEE FOLLOWING)

*One major employment record, showing chronology of promotion, as well as
increased level of responsibility through increased number of personnel involved.*

Amplified Resume   Clinton L. Seymour
                                                    -page 2-

EMPLOYMENT

1980-Present
APEX CAMERA CO.

1980

Employed in Tabulating Research Department, assigned to development of computer systems for payroll and production.

1982

Industrial Engineering Department. Assignments included office systems and methods, plant layout, production methods, and cost studies. Assignments based on accounting background included:

1. System of company gross profit shrinkage. Result: substantial reduction of loss by proper accounting methods, with major reduction in paperwork.

2. Efficiency study of cafeteria operations to minimize annual six-figure loss. Result: major reduction of loss to manageable level.

3. Coordinating and directing the relocation of Industrial Engineering Dept. Involved working with construction engineers, planning and timing move sequences so as to eliminate work interruption. Completed precisely on schedule.

1985

Moved to Photo Products Division, and promoted to department head of Inventory Control. Supervised 6 separate offices with 120 personnel, whose function was preparation of payroll, production control, in-process inventory records.

Department was disorganized due to transfer of previous department head. Met challenge. Streamlined operations, handled increased work load from production increases with same work force; boosted morale.

At request of Division Superintendent, prepared special cost analysis of old payroll reporting methods compared with cost of computer applications. Developed presentation which reached top-level management.

Promoted to present position of Personnel Director of Photo Products Division, with over 2,500 personnel. Handles employment of hourly workers through three assistants. Personally interviews and coordinates hiring of business and engineering personnel. Screens records, recommends promotions, makes decisions on upgrading.

References available

Synopsis of Resume of: 30 Sutton St.
ALAN L. THOMASON   Hattiesburg, MS 39401
                                                 Phone: (601) 761-4132

JOB OBJECTIVE

Position in field of Personnel, College Recruitment,
or College Relations

EMPLOYMENT

10/81-Present   DIRECTOR OF PLACEMENT AND ALUMNI RELATIONS
                 ASSISTANT DIRECTOR OF ADMISSIONS
                 Mississippi Southern College, Hattiesburg, MS

1980-1981   PURCHASING AGENT (resigned to accept better position
                 above)
                 Randolph Chemical Co., Butler, AL

1976-1979   Summers and part-time during college years:
                 Red Cross Swimming Instructor

EDUCATION

1971-1975   Allendale Preparatory School, Lake Charles, LA
                     Valedictorian of class; awarded year's scholarship
                     for European study and travel

1975-1979   University of Arkansas
                     Degree: B.S. in Social Sciences
                     Honors   Dean's List four times
                     Expenses: Earned approximately 75%.
                     Activities: President of: Junior and Senior class,
                                  Student Board of Governors, Inter-
                                  College Council of American Red Cross.
                                  Member of: Glee Club, Debating Team.

PERSONAL

Age: 25, married, health good.
Residence: College quarters; free to relocate.
Hobbies: Swimming; sailing; stamp collecting.
Affiliations: Southern College Personnel Officers Association;
               Mississippi State Deans & Guidance Counselors Associa-
               tion, Mississippi State Counselors Association

(FOR AMPLIFICATION SEE FOLLOWING)

Although shooting for industry, stress put on extraordinary accomplishments in
present position, demonstrating the energy and initiative obviously usable and
desirable in any field.

Amplified Resume

Alan L. Thomason
-page 2-

EMPLOYMENT HIGHLIGHTS

10/81-Present
MISSISSIPPI SOUTHERN COLLEGE

Originally employed as Assistant Director of Placement and Admissions. Promoted to present classification after one year.

As Director of Placement is responsible for senior and alumni placement, plus teacher placement and part-time and summer positions for undergraduates. In addition, does student advising and counseling, with job and ability evaluation.

As Assistant Director of Admissions, has set up a system of recruitment for the college. Gives talks before high school students and various other youth groups in the 15-county area, arousing and stimulating interest in Mississippi Southern College. Later, passes on qualifications of those who apply.

In placement field has made extensive contact with desirable companies; has built companies interviewing students from 75 to 120. Furthers this interest by speaking before various civic organizations. Keeps posted on requirements for a variety of fields and positions, then steers interviewers to right prospects. Entire program has been highly successful; relations with students and industry, excellent.

In newly created position of Director of Alumni Relations inaugurated a policy of regular contact; serves as liaison between alumni, faculty, and students.

Results have been positive.

(1) Dues-paying alumni percentage raised from 11% to 39%. National average is approximately 19%.

(2) Participation in insurance program benefiting college raised from 20% to 35%.

(3) Initiated a systematic contribution program supplementing the above.

General:

(1) Serves as Chairperson of Committee on Scholarship.

(2) Coordinates Graduate School studies; advises on financial aid available.

Reason for desiring change: Greater income.

References available

Synopsis of Resume of:
GRACE E. OSBORNE

5010 Sun Circle
Colorado Springs, CO 80907
Phone: (303) 457-4820

JOB OBJECTIVE

Fund-Raising

EMPLOYMENT

<u>1982</u>   Democratic Campaign Headquarters, General Election
        Fund-raising chairperson.

<u>1978-1982</u>   Colorado College, Colorado Springs, CO
        Director of Development

<u>Prior</u>   St. Mary's School for the Deaf, Buffalo, NY
        Director of Development
        State University of NY at Buffalo, NY
        Coordinator, Curriculum Development Center

VOLUNTEER EMPLOYMENT

1975-Present   Democratic Executive Committee.
        Precinct Capt., Steering Committee, State
        Convention Delegate, Vice-Chairperson,
        Political Action Committee.
        League of Women Voters.
        Board of Directors; Human Resources Chair-
        person; Project Director for Statewide Edu-
        cation Fund Conference; Coordinator for
        Equal Rights Amendment Ratification.

EDUCATION

1950   University of North Carolina, Greensboro, NC
        Degree: B.A. Sociology
1951   Merrill-Palmer Institute, Detroit, MI
        Graduate Study in Early Childhood Education

PERSONAL

Married; three self-supporting children. Health: excellent;
free to travel but not to relocate.

REFERENCES

Available on request

One page serves purpose here. Impressive background creates enough interest to
generate interview where details can be discussed.

Resume of
PAUL H. CARPENTER

149 Palmer Ave.
Des Moines, IA 50315
Phone: (515) 631-0551

JOB OBJECTIVE

Position as Insurance Specialist (Casualty, Fire, Marine) for banking real estate department, or position where extensive management experience can be fully utilized.

EMPLOYMENT

1972-1/85
MANAGER
Des Moines Casualty Insurance Co.

Employed as Underwriter. Approved or rejected business written for all forms of casualty insurance. Required expert knowledge of property evaluation, ability to judge past performance of individuals, and justify decision to salesperson and property owner if rejected. In four years promoted to Assistant Manager. In 1981 promoted to Manager. Duties similar with more responsibility inherent in Manager's spot.

Directed approximately 35 full-time employees; supervised efforts of 125 agents. Continuously recruited, encouraged, trained and worked with new personnel. Worked with agents through approximately six special agents in the office; was final authority on problems which persisted. Hired and trained office, clerical, and accounting personnel. Supervised prompt processing of applications and policies, and collection of delinquencies, and handled claims from insureds.

During term as Manager, company went through reorganization and top management change. Company policy dictated drastic cutbacks and economies in all offices, plus a change in representation policies. As a direct result of the latter, Des Moines office lost agencies, taking with them a substantial six-figure volume in premiums.

RECORD DURING MANAGEMENT PERIOD

More than regained loss above; has increased dollar volume. Properly and promptly handled and processed the increased volume, plus paperwork resulting from agency changes, with force of 15 compared with over 30 to start. Expanded full company services to the large area surrounding Des Moines, whereas only fire had been offered previously outside Polk County.

Reason for resignation: Impending transfer to undesirable location.

(continued)

1962-1972
PARTNER
Empire Insurers Agency, Des Moines, IA

With partner formed company. Acted as underwriter and office manager. Company dissolved when partner was forced to withdraw for
reasons of health.

1960-1962
UNDERWRITER
Bismarck Casualty & Surety Co., Bismarck, ND

Employed as clerk trainee; Promoted to underwriter, underwent extensive training and self-training program.

1962 transferred to Des Moines, Iowa, with larger responsibility.
Record was such invited by superior to join him in forming above
company. Resigned to do so.

EDUCATION

High school graduate; Underwriters Board courses in various phases
of insurance; numerous company courses in casualty, marine, and
general insurance.

PERSONAL

Age: Mature; married; five children--self-supporting.
Health: Good; no physical limitations.
Residence: Owns home; will relocate for exceptional opportunity.
Affiliations: Rotary Club; Chamber of Commerce.

REFERENCES

Available on request

*Synopsis page avoided in record of older man where last or present employment has
been of considerable duration. Immediate employment amplification serves to put
immediate focus on most significant aspect of record—namely, experience.*

Synopsis of Resume of: 3340 Brookmeade Dr.
LISA H. RYAN   Seattle, WA 98122
                                                 Phone: (206) 632-7000

JOB OBJECTIVE

Program specialist in private sector

EXPERIENCE

1983-Present   SEATTLE CENTRAL COMMUNITY COLLEGE, Seattle, WA
                     Program Specialist

1974-1983   LOWELL SCHOOL OF DESIGN, New York, NY
                     Assistant Director of Admissions

1972-1974   LUDLOW JR. HIGH SCHOOL, Ludlow, MA
                     Secondary Art Teacher

1968-1972   WARWICK PUBLIC SCHOOLS, Warwick, RI
                     Elementary Art Teacher

Other: Part-time to help defray cost of education: arts and
                crafts camp counselor; freelance artist; retail sales.

EDUCATION

1962-1968   Rhode Island School of Design, Providence, RI
                     Degree: B.F.A. in Graphic Arts Design

Other: Miscellaneous ongoing computer courses

PERSONAL

Born: 1944   Married, one son, good health, no physical limitations.
Hobbies: Painting; classical piano; reading.

(FOR AMPLIFICATION SEE FOLLOWING)

Amplified Resume   Lisa H. Ryan
                                                              -page 2-

EMPLOYMENT HIGHLIGHTS

<u>1983-Present</u>
<u>SEATTLE CENTRAL COMMUNITY COLLEGE</u>
Enrollment 10,000

As Program Specialist for the Center for Continuing Education and Community Center, general responsibilities encompass assisting with the
developing and marketing of the non-credit programming.

Writes copy and designs graphics for brochures and direct mail-outs;
plans publicity and coordinates advertising and photo assignments as
well as supervising photo production.

Specific responsibilities include: interviewing prospective teachers,
developing courses, acting as audiovisual coordinator, coordinating
seminars and special events.

<u>Reason for desiring change</u>: To enter private sector in position with
potential which will fully utilize diverse skills and experience.

<u>1974-1983</u>
<u>LOWELL SCHOOL OF DESIGN</u>

As Assistant Director of Admissions, did local and out-of-state recruitment. Interviewed prospective students; evaluated artistic abilities
and admission credentials. During tenure, applications rose over 50%,
enrollment 30%. Acted as Director of Admissions in Director's absence.
Hired, trained, and supervised staff of student aides. Salary increased
by approximately $9,000.

<u>Reason for leaving</u>: Husband's transfer.

<u>1968-1974</u>
<u>ART TEACHER</u>

Art teaching assignments in both elementary and secondary capacities
involved classroom teaching as well as responsibility for developing
art curricula and departmental budgets, and setting up various professional workshops.

REFERENCES

On Request

Synopsis of Resume of: 87 Puritan Rd.
GEOFFRY L. PFEFFER   Somerville, MA 02145
                                                Phone: (617) 988-5682

EMPLOYMENT

1980-Present   NEWCOMP, INC., Boston, MA ($200 million volume)
                        Regional Director

1966-1979   BANK OF BOSTON, Boston, MA
                        Systems Analyst Officer

EDUCATION

1962-1966   Stonehill College, N. Easton, MA
                        Degree: B.A. Major: Economics
                    American Institute of Banking
                        Effective Communication; Effective Analysis.
                    Seminars:
                        Effective Management; database concepts;
                        programming classes including IBM Cobol and
                        Assembler.

PERSONAL

Born: 1944   Married; four children; excellent health.
Hobbies: Chess; theater; reading; bridge; racket ball.

Affiliations: Association for Systems Management; Country Playhouse;
                    Community Chest; church-affiliated Mens' Service Club.

(FOR AMPLIFICATION SEE FOLLOWING)

At this level "Job Objective" need not be shown, giving latitude to submit record as
opportunities in field surface.

Amplified Resume

Geoffry L. Pfeffer
-page 2-

EMPLOYMENT HIGHLIGHTS

<u>1980-Present</u>
<u>NEWCOMP, INC.</u>
Employs 6,000 nationally; 2,500 locally.

Employed initially to design the deposit product of a project which is still under redesign due to some major architectural changes. Assistant Manager of team consisting of from two to ten persons, overseeing detailed functional and design phases.

Promoted to present position of Regional Director with salary raise in high five figures. In this capacity manages group of four business analysts who design and execute a test system for an integrated banking system. Has had marked success in CIF (Central Information File) and future expectation for Deposit CD (Certificate of Deposit) product.

Additionally, this group of analysts consults to the remainder of the corporation on banking situations.

<u>Reason for change</u>: Desires solid challenge beyond scope offered.

<u>1966-1979</u>
<u>BANK OF BOSTON</u>
17th largest assets in U.S.

Hired as Programmer Trainee, promoted to Systems Officer making recommendations to every department in bank. Worked on eight projects simultaneously, including automation of wire room services, improving work flow in proof and transit, and cost justification of new computer system.

<u>Reason for leaving</u>: Upward career move to improve status, scope, and challenge.

REFERENCES

Available in confidence following interview. Salary negotiable. Will relocate for right opportunity.

Synopsis of Resume of:
DAVID L. MC GRAW, Jr.

47 Beecher Place
Bangor, ME 04401
Phone: (207) 822-9177

JOB OBJECTIVE

Position as artist, designer, creative writer
for advertising or promotion work.
Industrial advertising or agency.

EMPLOYMENT

1982-6/85   MECHANICAL PASTE-UP IN DESIGN - Art Department
Langie Paper Container Corp., Bangor, ME

1980-1982   ADVERTISING MANAGER
Jewett Dept. Store, 29 Third St., Bangor, ME

1978-1980   FREELANCE - Augusta, Maine area.

1976-1978   CHIEF OF JEWELRY DESIGN
Best Arts, Inc., 900 Tremont Blvd., Bangor, ME

1974-1976   POSTER DESIGNER & RUBBER PLATE ENGRAVER
Porter Wells Inc., 308 Prince St., Boston, MA

Prior   Salem, Massachusetts:
  Becks Department Store - Assistant window trimmer
  Makin Advertising Agency - Layout, design, copywriting.
  Freer Photographers - Home photography.
(Left each job voluntarily to improve position.)

EDUCATION

1969-1972   Maryland Institute College of Art, Baltimore, MD
Left voluntarily for financial reasons.
  Courses included: Advertising Design, Photography,
Interior Decorating, Illustration, Life Drawing.

PERSONAL

Born: 2/17/51. No children. Health: excellent.
Hobbies: Painting; camping; fishing.
Affiliations: Board member Bangor Memorial Art Gallery.

(FOR AMPLIFICATION SEE FOLLOWING)

Field in which pictures and samples are literally more significant than a thousand resume words. Therefore resume merely points up training and experience indicating, wherever possible, samples of work available for review. To enclose or attach such samples could restrict opportunity to be invited for interview.

Amplified Resume   David L. McGraw, Jr.
                                                    -page 2-

<u>EMPLOYMENT HIGHLIGHTS</u>

1982-6/85
LANGIE PAPER CONTAINER CORP.
Mfrs.: cartons, packing containers

   Employed in Art Department to perform mechanical paste-up of designs
to be applied to packages, boxes, or cartons, primarily of food container type. In addition, assisted in actual package design.

   <u>Reason for leaving</u>: Business went bankrupt.

1980-1982
JEWETT DEPARTMENT STORE

   Employed as Advertising Manager. Prepared copy and art work. Did
layouts for news media selecting material of reader interest, and
slanting such material to acceptable style and store policy. Created and arranged store and window displays. Photographs of such
displays, and samples of newspaper ads are available for inspection.

   <u>Reason for leaving</u>: To accept position above which appeared to
offer greater potential.

1978-1980
FREELANCE

   Assisted established designers; obtained commissions on own (restaurant murals, portraits, etc.). Wrote several articles on fishing
and outdoor life (complete with photographs); had seven accepted for
national publication; available for review.

1976-1978
BEST ARTS, INC. (School pins, jewelry, etc.)

   Employed as head of jewelry design. Worked from written description
or rough sketch of desired article. Made and submitted accurate
formal drawing of item to school or organization for approval. Upon
acceptance, metal-die department used drawing for duplication.
Samples of work available. Resigned to do freelance work.

1974-1976
PORTER WELLS, INC.

   Employed as trainee in rubber plate engraving for reproduction of
posters. Made pencil drawings on tracing paper which was rubbed
down onto rubber plate and became guide to follow for hand cutting
with engraving tools. Progressed into original creative poster design. Resigned to gain additional experience in other art fields.

References on request

Synopsis of Resume of
LINDA KURTZ

155 Oakville Ave.
Rye, NY 10580
Phone: (716) 555-9862;
Home: 867-5493

JOB OBJECTIVE

Fashion Coordinator

EXPERIENCE

1977-Present   HENTLEY DEPARTMENT STORE, NY
                 Fashion Coordinator

1976-1977   Sakowitz, Houston, TX
                 Co-owner bridal shop

1974-1976   Kentall Modeling School, Pittsburgh, PA
                 Model and Teacher

1972-1974   WJZ-TV, Baltimore, MD
                 Weather reporter, television commercials

Prior   Freelance modeling (London, Paris)

EDUCATION

1966-1970   Northwestern University
                    Major: Advertising (Business Administration)
                    Minor: Applied Arts

Other: Fluent French; working knowledge Spanish.

PERSONAL

Born: 1948. Single. Health: Excellent.
Finances: Good order; owns home, car, beach property.
Hobbies: Water sports; sculpting (clay, metal); pottery;
                 fashion research.
Affiliations: Art League; Red Flat Charette (Environmental Organiza-
                 tion)

(FOR AMPLIFICATION SEE FOLLOWING)

*Heavy experience divided into major categories of fashion interest to prevent its
being clouded in the sea of detail inherent in highly detailed work of fashion
consulting.*

Amplified Resume

EMPLOYMENT HIGHLIGHTS

<u>1977-Present</u>
<u>HENTLEY DEPARTMENT STORE</u>

Employed as fashion coordinator for leading NYC department store, with responsibilities centered in four major areas: fashion, display, training, public relations.

<u>Fashion</u> -- Full responsibility for eight to ten major fashion shows a year, plus smaller in-store shows, and shows organized for various community organization functions.

Hires models, selects clothes appropriate to season or theme, meets with buyers and display personnel to communicate needs for lighting, decorating, music, and amplification. Supervises rehearsals and delivers commentary on day of show. At show conclusion, writes model vouchers, checks merchandise return to store; evaluates gains made in increased sales.

<u>Display</u> -- Responsible for "Front and Forward," a program devised to present unified look to store by coordinating all displays, cases, and T-stands.

<u>Training</u> -- On own initiative set up training program for all ready-to-wear sales personnel. Daily departmental meetings to familiarize salespersons with featured advertised merchandise in daily papers and to point up unique selling points of stocks. Bimonthly fashion meetings with focus on total store fashion message and inventory.

<u>Public Relations</u> -- Organizes and implements store's seasonal holiday breakfasts and brunches given periodically throughout the year for general public.

Responsible for store's annual Sewing Contest. Follows entries through to final judging. Does commentary and presents final awards.

Writes publicity releases; does public speaking at women's clubs; occasional radio and television appearances.

<u>Reason for desiring change</u>: To improve status and income.

REFERENCES

On request. Do not contact present employer now.

Resume of:
KIM CARTER

3762 North Florida Ave.
Lakeland, FL 33805
Phone: (813) 365-4554

OBJECTIVE

Television Commercials; Modeling; Dinner Theater

PERSONAL

Actress/Singer/Dancer/Model. Height 5'6"; Weight 108; green eyes; chestnut hair; S.A.G. eligible. Excellent Health, unencumbered; free to travel or relocate anywhere in U.S., Canada, or Mexico.

EXPERIENCE

T.V. RADIO CREDITS:
National
New Weight Diet Wafer (solo commercial); Lovely Panty Hose, Pro Tennis Shoes (national).

Local
Tim Kantor Show (one-woman Gershwin show); Jeff Arthur Productions (jingles); "Jaques Brel" (filmed for TV as live theater). Radio and TV commercials.

THEATER

Champlain Valley Shakespeare Festival, Burlington, VT.
    "As You Like It"; "The Tempest."
Goodman Repertory Company, Chicago IL.
    "Heartbreak House"; "Dutchman."
Royal Tyler Theatre, Burlington, VT.
    "The Man Who Came to Dinner"; "Three Sisters"; "Born Yesterday";
    "Cat on a Hot Tin Roof"; "Death of Bessie Smith."
Monomoy Summer Theater, Cape Cod.
    "Cabaret"; "Sabrina"; "Skin of Our Teeth"; "Charlie's Aunt."
St. Mark's Place Theatre Ensemble, NYC.
    "The Contrast"; "Sweet Bird of Youth."
TGL Theatre, Burlington, VT.
    Writer and choreographer of original Gershwin Revue.

CLUB PERFORMANCES

Bottom Line Cabaret Theatre; Blue Garter Cabaret; Knickerbocker Saloon; The Blue Note (NYC). Big Band lead vocals with Casey & Company, New England tour (songs of the thirties and forties).

One-woman musicals for various local clubs and organizations.

(continued)

EDUCATION

Oberlin Conservatory of Music; Master's in Theater, University of South Florida. Studied dance under Holby Grethe. NYC; acting under Jerry Roth.

Additional skills: Artist; lyricist, jingle-writer; copywriter.

IMMEDIATE AVAILABILITY. Call answering service anytime.

Synopsis of Resume of
SUSAN WAYNE

3978 Sandringham Drive
Atlanta, GA 30305
Phone: (414) 233-0875

OBJECTIVE

Position in communications that would utilize educational major
and current experience

EMPLOYMENT

1983-Present   WEAT-TV, Atlanta, GA
                      Assistant Traffic Director
                      Camera assistant

Part-time   Sarasota Board of Education, FL
1980-1982   Classroom aide in Headstart Program
                    Maas Department Store, Sarasota, FL
                      Sales, window dressing, modeling

EDUCATION

1976-1980   Florida State University, Tallahassee, FL
                    Degree:
                      Bachelor of Arts.
                    Major:
                      Mass Communications.

PERSONAL

                    Single. Health: excellent.
Hobbies: Water sports; tennis; sewing; amateur theater.
Affiliations: YWCA; Community Theater; Civic Music Association.

(FOR AMPLIFICATION SEE FOLLOWING)

*Anxious to get foot in door of larger-market television studio; consequently avoided
specific objective that would narrow opportunity for being considered for any
possible opening.*

Amplified Resume   Susan Wayne
                                                    -page 2-

EMPLOYMENT

July 1983-Present

Employed as general clerk at station WEAT-TV. Duties consisted of
general office work, filling in at receptionist's desk, filing and
checking logs in the Traffic Department.

After four months was promoted to assistant Traffic Director. Duties
involved creating a television log; procuring sales availabilities
for the sales department; organizating and preparing billing information for the bookkeeping department. In addition, pulled and
distributed teletype data, contacted syndicators and distributors
of taped shows and films to insure proper scheduling and playdates.
Prepared advance program information for television publications.

In addition, was given responsibility for organizing the film department during interim period from resignation of film director
until replacement was located. Trained the replacement in innova-
tive film handling and shipping procedures, resulting in vastly
improved, streamlined film department.

Assisted in production of commercials, have appeared on camera for
several taped commercials; have operated camera on both live and
taped local shows. Have written copy and done voice-overs.

Reason for leaving:

Wish to relocate in larger market area.

REFERENCES

Available on Request

Synopsis of Resume of: 865 Bannaker Way, #5
PEGGY PAGE   Montgomery, AL 36195
                                          Phone: (205) 366-7652

OBJECTIVE

General Assignment Reporter or Area Correspondent

EXPERIENCE

1982-Present   MONTGOMERY PRESS, Montgomery, AL; Circulation 50,000.
                    Reporter - from copy clerk.

1980-1982   COVINGTON HERALD, Covington, LA; Circulation 14,000
                    Assistant Editor

Other: Editor of high school and college newspapers.

EDUCATION

1979   University of Alabama, Tuscaloosa, Alabama
                    Degree: BA in Journalism.
                    Minor: Political Science.
                    Honors: Dean's List; Editor newspaper.

PERSONAL

Age: 28; single; excellent health; free to relocate.
Hobbies: Tennis; swimming; reading; writing.
Skills: Word processor; 35mm and 120 Rolex; photo sizing and
           cropping; paste-up; proofing; editing; headlines.

EMPLOYMENT HIGHLIGHTS:

As Assistant Editor for small weekly newspaper, gained good foundation
in mechanics of putting paper together, meeting deadlines, and use of
word processor. Wrote general news items when time permitted. Left
to accept position with greater salary and more reporter assignments.

Starting as copy clerk, advanced to general assignment reporter covering
hard news, including City Council, School Board, and various community
interest meetings. Does personality/celebrity interviews on special
photo/journal assignments. Fills in for entertainment editor on occasion.

REFERENCES: On request. Portfolio available for review.

Combining both synopsis and employment detail on a one-page resume which
adequately serves in view of short record, pointing up nonetheless a variety of
specific, usable skills.

Synopsis of:
MICHAEL SIMMONS

6440 Oregon St.
Ft. Myers, FL 33901
Phone: (813) 297-5590

JOB OBJECTIVE

PRODUCTION MANAGER

1981-Present	Production Manager WXLF-TV, Ft. Myers, FL
1979-1981	Production Manager WAEO, Rhinelander, WI
1975-1978	Chief, Information Division United States Army
Part-time	Summer jobs: Radiographer, Pipeweld X-ray Corp. Freelance copywriting with advertising firms.

EDUCATION

| 1969-1973 | Syracuse University, Syracuse, NY
   Degree: B.S. in Broadcasting |
| Other: | Northeast Broadcasting School, Boston, MA |

PERSONAL

Born:	1950. Married; two children; health--excellent.
Hobbies:	Writing; woodworking; music; golf.
Affiliations:	Writers Club; Palmaire Golf Club.

(FOR AMPLIFICATION SEE FOLLOWING)

Amplified Resume   Michael Simmons
                                                    -page 2-

EMPLOYMENT HIGHLIGHTS

June 1981-Present
WXLF-TV, Ft. Myers, FL

Employed as Production Manager of new television station not yet
on the air. Had full responsibility for initial airdate preparation; in full charge of all production following airdate. Included:
newscasts, commercial announcements, programs, and administrative
details.

Due to small staff, assumed additional duties of program director,
continuity writer, staff announcer, as well as assisting cameramen.
Despite understaffing and limited technical equipment, organized
an efficient, smooth-running unit resulting in the new station
moving up in national network ratings well beyond the expectations
for a new station in a comparable time period.

Reason for desiring change: Prefer larger, established station,
where efforts may be concentrated in production area.

January 1979-June 1981
WAEO, Rhinelander, WI

Hired as continuity writer; promoted in two months to Production
Director. Had full responsibility for all commercial production
and attendant details.

Reason for leaving: Amicable separation to accept present position.

1975-1978
United States Army

Chief, Information Division; qualified in one-third normal time due
to self-training on own time and initiative. Special accomplishments included:
(1) Wrote, narrated, filmed, and directed half-hour color documen-
    tary.
(2) Provided news releases; filmed and supplied news film to
    national news services.
(3) Had sole responsibility for any news released.

REFERENCES

On request

Synopsis of Resume of: 9972 Lone Tree
PATRICIA KENT   Dallas, TX 75218
                                               Phone: (214) 382-4391

JOB OBJECTIVE

Public Affairs Director

EMPLOYMENT

1983-Present	Public Affairs Director; talk show hostess; reporter WXTN-TV, Dallas, TX
1980-1983	WYND, Slidell, LA Traffic and continuity director
1978-1980	WQED-TV, Houston, TX Production Assistant
1975-1978	WVIZ, Cleveland, OH Continuity and production

EDUCATION

1971-1975	Ohio State University Major: Journalism Minor: Communications media
Other:	New York University Summer workshop in radio and television Dallas Advertising Club Public Relations Seminar
Languages:	Spanish (fluent), French (working knowledge)

PERSONAL

Age:	33; Single; health: excellent.
Hobbies:	Swimming; scuba; sewing; puppetry; art; painting.
Affiliations: (present)	Dallas Press Club; Museum Director; Ecology Committee; Professional Women's Club.

(FOR AMPLIFICATION SEE FOLLOWING)

Although jobs frequently changed, progression in salary and responsibilities make logical sequence. Emphasis on affiliations to strengthen qualifications for objective.

Amplified Resume   Patricia Kent
                                                         -page 2-

EMPLOYMENT

1983-Present
WXNT-TV, Dallas TX

Employed as member of News Department assigned to special features.
Included civic and cultural events, politics, and soft news items.
Required to shoot, process, and edit film, write and produce audio
commentary.

Upon resignation of talk show host, was given opportunity to be
hostess of the live show station presented daily as a public relations and community project. Given full responsibility for the
hour show. Designed set, created opening and close, procured
clothing sponsor to furnish daily wardrobe, lined up and scheduled
all guests. Guests are briefed slightly, but prefers spontaneity
of the largely unrehearsed interview. Guests have included: U.S.
senators, visiting actors and celebrities, as well as concerned
citizens within the station's viewing area.

Recently given title of "Public Affairs Director"; responsibilities
in addition to those above include moderating panel discussions and
special programs on various issues.

Reason for desiring change: Salary not in line with increased
responsibilities.

1980-1983
WYND, Slidell, LA

Employed as receptionist with agreement for transfer to production
department when vacancy occurred. An earlier opening in traffic
department offered and accepted. Responsible for daily log as
well as continuity; wrote commercial copy and station promotional
material. In addition, did occasional on-air spots and voice-overs;
filled in for "talk show" hostess when needed. Left for better
position.

1978-1980
WQED-TV (Educational)

Employed as production assistant, designed sets and graphics; served
as liaison between the technical and instructional personnel. Left
for better-paying job above.

1975-1978

Employed as production assistant for the city's then new educational
television station. Duties proved to be primarily in the traffic
area (daily logs and program guides). Amicable separation to seek
position with more production emphasis.

REFERENCES ON REQUEST

Synopsis of Resume of: 33 Rand Place
NANCY W. MITCHELL   Atlanta, GA 30315
             Phone: (404) 897-9641

<u>JOB OBJECTIVE</u>

Field of Public Relations - Promotion - Advertising

<u>EDUCATION</u>

1974-1978   Mt. Holyoke College, South Hadley, MA
      Degree: A.B. Major: English.
      Assistant Editor college publication.

Other: "Experiment in International Living" - six weeks. 1974.
      Competitive program. Selection of young Americans
      to represent U.S. in foreign countries. Selection
      on basis of: scholastic achievement, physical fit-
      ness, personality, and character. Assigned to group
      going to France; spent six weeks with French family.

      Has traveled extensively; speaks French fluently.

<u>EMPLOYMENT</u>

11/80-Present KYKA-TV, 890 So. Main St., Atlanta, GA
      Promotion Writer with multiple additional responsibil-
      ities.

10/78-11/79 MATHER ADVERTISING, INC. Radio and TV Advertising
      70 Stone St., Boston, MA
      Secretarial and general office work.

<u>PERSONAL</u>

Born: 1/20/56. Single. Health: excellent.
Hobbies: Tennis; golf; music (accomplished pianist).
Residence: Apartment; willing to relocate anywhere in U.S.

(FOR AMPLIFICATION SEE FOLLOWING)

*Field in which superior education is likely to carry more weight than average
experience would; therefore, former is given synopsis page preference.*

Amplified Resume   Nancy W. Mitchell
                                                       -page 2-

EMPLOYMENT

1980-Present
KYKA-TV, Atlanta, GA

Promotion writer responsible for all on-the-air promotion (30 sec.,
60 sec., etc.) for each day's log. Spots and promotions are extensive, requiring speed and good organization in meeting deadlines,
in addition to creative writing ability. Responsible for all
trailers, tapes, slides, and videotape. Checks and processes them
on arrival; screens them for use. Determines what will be used,
discarded, or cut; instructs film department on proper cutting
procedure to attain desired length and content.

In clerical area, logs all promotional announcements, checks traffic
boards and maintains Kardex file. Makes out promotion orders, promotion reports, program schedules, and distributes to proper departments. Makes periodic program checks to insure information is
correct and current.

Reason for desiring change: Feels duties too general; would like
position with more clearly defined responsibilities.

10/78-11/79
MATHER ADVERTISING, INC., Boston, MA

Employed for secretarial and office work. In short period responsibilities broadened to include radio and television copy and
limited account servicing. Office packaged several shows affording
opportunity to gain valuable experience in this area, in addition
to public relations and agency media work.

Reason for leaving: To improve status.

REFERENCES AVAILABLE

Resume of: 3897 Jay St.
L. ROBERT BAUMAN   Rochester, NY 14611
                                              Phone: (716) 733-8120

JOB OBJECTIVE

Public Relations - Public Information

EXPERIENCE

1980-Present
MONROE COUNTY PUBLIC SCHOOLS, Rochester, NY

Accepted position as Public Information Officer of the county school
system, working directly under Superintendent of Schools, who reports
to the Board of Education.

Duties encompass: writing, editing, coordinating graphics of four
periodicals. (1) Quarterly newspaper -- 40,000 distribution. (2)
Monthly report on a specific school, together with activities and
pictures -- 4,000 distribution. (3) Biweekly internal newsletter.
(4) Annual School Board Report -- 120,000 distribution.

Writes, hosts, and produces biweekly television program spotlighting
personnel, activities, and achievements of individual students to increase parental and public awareness of local school system.

Acts as liaison between the School Board, various media, United Way,
and the Disaster Preparedness Office. Does considerable public speaking as requested by community organizations.

Directly responsible for the management of the Public Information
Office, which includes personnel, budget, printing, and distribution
of the periodicals.

Would make change to warmer climate.

1965-1980
LEE COUNTY BOARD OF INSTRUCTION, Ft. Myers, Florida

Accepted position as instrumental classroom music teacher immediately
following college graduation. Selected as "One of the Outstanding
Teachers in America" and promoted to department supervisor. Co-authored
"Elementary Music Curriculum Guide" and selected as guest clinician at
state "Early Childhood and Elementary Education Conference."

1965-1980 (summers)

Hosted two-hour classical music program over WZAY radio during July
and August, five mornings a week.

(continued)

L. Robert Bauman
-page 2-

EDUCATION

1961-1965   University State Teachers College, Crane Music School.
             Potadam, NY.
             Degree: B.S. in Music Education

PERSONAL

Born: 1941; married; two children in college; health excellent.
Hobbies: Piano; barbershop chorus singing; family activities.

REFERENCES

Available

Unusual field and qualifications do not lend themselves to synopsis treatment as effectively as hitting the story head-on.

Synopsis of Resume of: 23 Antlers Dr.
FRANK L. PALMER   Lake Bluff, IL 60044
                                           Phone: (309) 629-5742

OBJECTIVE

Training Position in Computer Programming
where education in field can be utilized

EMPLOYMENT

1980-Present	HYDROMETER CALIBRATOR - Instrument Assembler. American Optical Co., Lake Bluff, IL
Prior	Part-time and summer employments prior to service. (Note: has been gainfully employed from early youth, financially assisting widowed mother and defraying full cost of education.)

EDUCATION

1974	Hayes High School, Hayes, KS Awarded scholarship to Institute below
1975	Wichita Institute of Technology, Wichita, KS Emphasis on college level math; left voluntarily to enter service.
Current	Computer Center, Lake Bluff, IL. Programming courses taken include: COBOL, ALC, and FORTRAN. Operations courses include: Introduction to E.D.P., Advanced Operating Systems, and RPG II.
Service 1976-1980	U.S. Navy. Seaman Recruit to Dental Technician 1/c. Honorable discharge; no reserve obligation.

PERSONAL

Age: 28	Single. Good Health. Willing to relocate.
Hobbies:	Sports in general; stamp collecting.
Affiliations:	Men's Civic Club; Lions Club; church member.

(FOR AMPLIFICATION SEE FOLLOWING)

Resume for trainee applicant stressing self-starting qualities, among the most looked-for qualification in trainees.

Amplified Resume   Frank L. Palmer
                                                         -page 2-

EMPLOYMENT HIGHLIGHTS

1980-Present
AMERICAN OPTICAL COMPANY
Manufacturer temperature and other precision instruments.

   Originally employed in sub and final assembly of various instruments; in six months transferred to hydrometer calibration. Works
   alone in the activity. Begins with bare instrument of various
   sizes; uses several basic fluids at controlled temperatures, using
   mathematical interpolations to fit scales into tubes for proper
   reading with various solutions.

   Except for special rush and/or emergency orders, sets own work pattern. To eliminate bottlenecks due to lack of essential supplies,
   has learned to operate glass tube and bulb producing machinery and,
   when necessary, produces own supplies.

   Excellent relations with co-workers and superiors. Company's
   appreciation of worth indicated by increase in yearly salary of
   $3,000.

   Reason for desiring change: Has self-trained for position in growing computer field; would make change (to utilize this preparation)
   to progressive company offering salary commensurate with ability to
   produce.

GENERAL

   Entirely on own initiative, began and continues computer programming
   training.

   Instruction has included actual operation of various machines, as
   well as programming experience. Marks ranged from "A" to "B plus."
   Plans to continue data processing studies as employment permits.

REFERENCES

   On request

Synopsis of Resume of: 879 Wiltshire Rd.
MELVIN J. HAMILTON   Lowell, MA 01835
                                                 Phone: (617) 986-4966

JOB OBJECTIVE

Programming or supervisory position

EMPLOYMENT RECORD

1980-present   Coordinating and Scheduling Analyst
                Martin Co., Lowell, MA (Mfr. of helicopters)

1976-1980   Systems Analyst
                Curtiss Electronics Corp. (Mfr. electronic equipment)
                  Boston, MA

1974-1976   Group Leader (Computer Operations)
                General Copy Corp., Boston, MA; left for better position
                  above.

1971-1974   Senior Computer Operator
                Newark Power Co., Newark, NJ; left for better position
                  above.

EDUCATION

1967-1970   University of Rochester, Rochester, NY
                  B.S. Degree.

1971   Certificate of Graduation, Computer Learning Center,
                  New Jersey. Courses in Programming and Operations.
                  Proficient in COBOL, Assembly, and FORTRAN languages.

PERSONAL

Born: 1949. Married, four children; good health.
Hobbies: Sailing; bridge; boat building.
Affiliations: Lowell Yacht Club; Chamber of Commerce; U of R Alumni
                Association
Service: Member National Guard.

(FOR AMPLIFICATION SEE FOLLOWING)

Amplified Resume   Melvin J. Hamilton
                                                         -page 2-

                              EMPLOYMENT

1980-present
MARTIN CO.

    Employed as Coordinating and Scheduling Analyst with following
    responsibilities: projecting future machine schedules, coordinating
    new systems in operations sections, explaining new procedures to
    operating sections.

    Helped install a new numbering system for reports and machine runs;
    assigned reports and run number to new, recurring, or one-time job.
    Required to have full knowledge of each system as to operation and
    purpose.

    Duties included statistical work for operations supervisor. Devel-
    oped figures for management (budget, rental, machine usage, etc.).

    Indication of company evaluation: $4000 per year increase in
    salary.

    Reason for desiring change: to be discussed at interview.

1976-1980
CURTISS ELECTRONICS CORP.

    Employed as Systems Analyst. Developed system for customer require-
    ments; priced system for profitable, successful bid. Wrote customer
    contracts; attended bidders' conferences.

    Followed operations closely to insure fulfillment of contractual re-
    quirements. Made monthly financial evaluations of each contract;
    evaluated existing systems.

    Reason for leaving: Offer from Martin Co., which appeared to have
    greater potential.

                              REFERENCES

                              Available

Synopsis of Resume of: 110 Summer St.
ARNOLD BAXTER   Los Angeles, CA 90057
                                                         Phone: (213) 542-2114

<u>JOB OBJECTIVE</u>

Computer Department Supervisor

<u>EMPLOYMENT</u>

1981-Present   HILL MANUFACTURING CO.
                 874 Castille St., Los Angeles, CA
                 Department Supervisor

1972-1980   EASTERN OIL COMPANY, 502 Madison Ave., New York, NY
                 Computer Operator in Saudi Arabia.

1965-1972   WORLD CHEMICAL CORP., Newark, NJ
                 Computer Operator
                 (Moved up from stock clerk)

Prior   LITTLESTONE STEEL CO., Hamilton Ontario, Canada
                 Miscellaneous duties (part-time and summer employment)

<u>EDUCATION</u>

1978   Diploma, Computer Learning Center, New York City.
                    Courses in Programming (COBOL, ALC, FORTRAN);
                    Operations (Operating Systems); RPG II;
                    Management. Ranked second in class of thirty-four.

<u>PERSONAL</u>

Age: 36   Single. Health: good. Free to relocate.
Hobbies: Football (participation and spectator); reading.
Affiliations: American Machine Accounting Association.

(FOR AMPLIFICATION SEE FOLLOWING)

Company name given precedence over position title, as companies are well known.
This gives position added importance, indicating larger operation responsibility. In
lieu of formal education, determination for self-education emphasized.

Amplified Resume   Arnold Baxter
                                                     -page 2-

EMPLOYMENT HIGHLIGHTS

1981-Present
HILL MANUFACTURING CO.
(Industrial textile, interior trim)

Originally employed as Computer Operator. Department composed of
fifteen persons (including time-recording clerks); was inefficiently
run. In six weeks was promoted to Department Supervisor, and
directed to bring it into full usefulness.

Replaced obsolete machines, eliminating two verifiers, reduced work
force from fifteen to ten. Retrained entire group, replaced unsuit-
able personnel, hired more effective operators.

Reduced force handles 43 applications including: Accounts Receivable and Payable, Payroll, Labor Analysis, Cost of Sales, Inventory
Control, Customer Mailings, Reports, all time-recording operations.

Company operations have increased over 28%; over 450 personnel are
employed; branch has been added in Canada; one is in formation in
the East. Computer work for branch plants, as well as main plant,
is performed in Los Angeles. Operation is smooth, employee relations good. Only reason for change would be to take over a larger
operation. Yearly income has increased by over $20,000 since 1981.

1972-1980
EASTERN OIL COMPANY

Employed on four-year contract as Computer Operator in Saudi Arabia,
a major installation with all types of equipment up to computers.
Moved up to supervision of material order and supply system for this
district. This meant a weekly balance of all items required by the
district. Contract renewed for second four-year period. Resigned
after completion of second contract to return to normal living conditions.

1965-1972
WORLD CHEMICAL CORP.

Employed as stock clerk, took leave of absence to complete high
school. Returned as Computer Operator; operated all types of equipment until resigned in 1972 to accept highly paid overseas position.

REFERENCES

Available

Synopsis of Resume of: 418 Delancey Place
JOSEPH MORGAN   Omaha, NB 61855
Certified Public Accountant   Phone: (402) 739-2331

JOB OBJECTIVE

Treasurer or Controller with medium-sized company

EMPLOYMENT

1984-Present   TREASURER and DIRECTOR (of both company and subsidiary)
                Henry Morris Co., Omaha, NB
                Lincoln Machinery Co., Lincoln, NB

1976-1984   VICE PRESIDENT, CONTROLLER, SECRETARY
                Bloomington Perforating Co., St. Paul, MN

1973-1976   SENIOR ACCOUNTANT in Public Accounting firm.
                In charge of audits and tax work.
                Richard Moriarty & Co., C.P.A., Chicago, IL

1970-73   PUBLIC ACCOUNTING
                James Platt, C.P.A., Chicago, IL

EDUCATION

1969-1973   University of Chicago
                    Degree: B.S.
                    Major: Accounting; "A" average

1967-1969   Florida Technical Institute, Jacksonville, FL
                    One year full-time; balance evenings.

PERSONAL

Born: 3/2/47. Married; no children; health: good.
Affiliations: Midwest Chapter C.P.A.; National Institute, C.P.A.
Service: U.S. Navy Seaman Recruit to Lt. (jg)
                Honorably released; no reserve obligation.

(FOR AMPLIFICATION SEE FOLLOWING)

*Normally company dollar volume can be used as indicator of level of accounting
responsibilities. In this instance company volume was so small it was omitted in favor
of number of employees.*

Amplified Resume

EMPLOYMENT HIGHLIGHTS

1984-Present
HENRY MORRIS CO. (200 employees)
Multi-plant manufacturer of corrugated or fiber box machinery

As Treasurer and Director of the company and subsidiary (Lincoln Machinery Co.), has control of all accounting, company financing, and all employees in these fields.

Results:
By system changes has improved and speeded informative and permanent records, while reducing clerical and administrative salaries by $100,000 per annum. Assisted in increasing profits; company financial strength has increased substantially.

Reason for change: Desires post with larger company offering remuneration commensurate with responsibilities.

1976-1984
BLOOMINGTON PERFORATING CO.
Perforated metal (75 employees)

Originally employed as Controller. Promoted to Vice President, Controller, and Secretary. Had full charge of all accounting operations and personnel. Consulted on financial aspects of business.

Results:
Company experienced period of successful operation and growth.

Reason for change: To accept better position with larger company.

REFERENCES

Available on request

Synopsis of Resume of: 35 Fountain St.
LOUIS GLEESON   Elgin, IL 60102
                                                 Phone: (312) 793-5357

OBJECTIVE

Position in Accounting utilizing supervisory experience.
Potential with long-term benefits.

EXPERIENCE

1980-Present   BROOKSIDE CLUB & RESTAURANT, Elgin, IL
                    Night Auditor

1970-1979   GARDEN PHOTO ENGRAVING CO., INC., Mineola, NY
                    Business Manager - Corporate Director.
                    Company liquidated.

EDUCATION

Hofstra University, Hempstead, NY
Major: Business/Bookkeeping/Accounting

Skills: Various computer systems, typewriter.

PERSONAL

Born: 1945; single; health--excellent; free to relocate.
Hobbies: Ice skating; fishing; spectator sports.
Affiliations: Administrative Management Society.

(FOR AMPLIFICATION SEE FOLLOWING)

*"Displaced" by virtue of long-term employment termination and decision to move to
new area and start anew. Is overqualified for present position, which is consequently
given short shrift.*

Amplified Resume

Louis Gleeson
-page 2-

EMPLOYMENT HIGHLIGHTS

January 1980-Present

Accepted interim position as night auditor for large, prestigious club. Responsible for auditing all customer tickets for food and beverage daily. Reads out the cash registers and balances sales for the day to register readout. Writes up daily report of all business transacted for that day.

Reason for desiring change:
Eager for better-paying position with long-term benefits more in line with heavy experience in accounting and supervision.

1970-1979
GARDEN PHOTO ENGRAVING CO., INC.

Accepted position as Administrative Assistant following honorable discharge from the Air Force.

Promoted to General Business Manager responsible for all finances of the corporation: banking, accounts receivable and payable, taxes, as well as for government classified material.

Bonded, with SECRET Security Clearance, dictated correspondence, supervised bookkeeper, credit manager, and clerks. Kept detailed records of sales; balanced all books monthly. Instituted and managed computer system used by accounting department.

Steady raise in salary from initial $8,000 to high five figures.

Reason for leaving:
Company liquidated. Made decision to relocate to Illinois and establish permanent residence.

REFERENCES

Please do not contact present employer until after interview.

Synopsis of Resume of:
GORDON T. WAGNER

84 Welling Avenue
Richmond, VA 23225
Phone: (703) 262-4876

JOB OBJECTIVE

Credit Supervision

EMPLOYMENT

6/82-Present   ABC TEXTILES, INC. (2,000 plus employees)
Richmond, VA
     Assistant Credit Manager

8/78-6/82   CONSOLIDATED FOODS, INC. (1,000 employees)
Elizabeth City, VA
     Credit Manager

Prior   Part-time during college and summers:
     Milo Manse, CPA, Palo Alto, CA

EDUCATION

9/74-6/78   Stanford University, Palo Alto, CA
     Degree: B.S. in Business Administration   Major:
     Accounting
     Honors: Graduated Cum Laude.
     Activities: Debating; Honorary Business Fraternity.

Miscellaneous   University of Richmond, Richmond, VA
     Course sponsored by National Credit Foundation.

PERSONAL

Born: 1956. Single. Health: excellent.
Residence: Owns home; will relocate for proper opportunity.
Hobbies: Skeet; horseback riding.
Affiliations: National Association of Credit Men; Nat. Rifle Asso-
     ciation
Civic: Volunteers accounting services to various civic
     organizations.

(FOR AMPLIFICATION SEE FOLLOWING)

*Both major employments for nationally known companies; therefore, company name
given precedence over position title. Rather than divulge company figures, applicant
shows results of effort company evaluation as indicated by salary more than doubling
during employment.*

Amplified Resume   Gordon T. Wagner
                                                       -page 2-

EMPLOYMENT

1982-Present
ABC TEXTILES, INC.

Employed in present capacity to assume full authority in extension
of credit and supplemental handling of a substantial portion of
company's prospective and actual accounts. Total credit in substantial seven figures. Accounts made up of textile wholesalers
and are located throughout the entire United States, Canada, Mexico,
and South America. Consequently, thorough knowledge of foreign as
well as domestic credit problems is required and essential.

Grants credit on basis of financial statements and past credit
record. For single accounts, amounts often reach figures exceeding
customer's net worth. Representing so major a creditor necessitates
acting as advisor to the customer firm or business on policies and
procedures. Results of assistance have proved successful; advice
is constantly sought and readily accepted.

Supervises ten members of credit department in details of credit
work; has full authority when accounts become delinquent. Works
closely with sales force; prospects for likely accounts which are
suggested to sales. Notifies salespeople of trouble areas. Since
credit is geared to assist, not hamper sales by excessive caution,
sound judgment is required.

In general, develops special approaches to trouble areas. Knows and
is known to management of hundreds of companies throughout North and
South America.

Salary has more than doubled during employment with ABC.

Reason for desiring change: Wants top credit spot not probable in
present company for several years.

8/78-6/82
CONSOLIDATED FOODS, INC.

Employed as Credit Clerk, promoted to Assistant Credit Manager to
Credit Manager.

Work and responsibilities similar to above on smaller scale.
Accounts (all domestic), included: jobbers, distributors, wholesale
groceries.

Reason for leaving: To accept better-paying position, and to broad-
en experience with larger company above.

References available on request.

Synopsis of Resume of: 304 Sutton Pl.
LYNN ZIMMERMAN   Des Moines, IA 50311
                                                Phone: (515) 982-7650

JOB OBJECTIVE

Position in Banking leading to Consumer Lending

EMPLOYMENT

1982-5/85   SAVINGS COUNSELOR
                     Midland Savings & Loan, Kansas City, KS
                     Resigned due to husband's transfer.

1979-9/82   SUPERVISING TELLER, from Management Trainee
                     United Jersey Midstate Bank, Aberdeen, NJ
                     Resigned because of husband's transfer.

EDUCATION

1974-1978   Rosemont College, Rosemont, PA
                     B.A. Major - Business Administration

Other: Night courses in: computer operations; word process-
                 int; effective communication.

PERSONAL

Age: 27   Married; no children; excellent health.
Hobbies: Aerobics; golf; needlepoint.
Affiliations: Toastmistress Club; Girl Scouts.

(FOR AMPLIFICATION SEE FOLLOWING)

Resume technique for handling employment changes because of geographical spouse
transfers.

Amplified Resume   Lynn Zimmerman
                                                       -page 2-

EMPLOYMENT HIGHLIGHTS

1982-1985
MIDLAND SAVINGS AND LOAN

Employed as Savings Counselor in large savings and loan institution
with assets over $1,470 million, and 400 employees.

Charged with responsibility of explaining the several types of savings
plans and counseling as to most feasible plan. Opened new accounts
with all attendant paperwork, making certain procedures were totally
understood to avoid any future misunderstandings.

Customer problem solving was integral part of the position, requiring
patience, good humor, and thorough grasp of general banking.

Opened over 700 new accounts during tenure; salary raised by 40%. Resigned due to husband's transfer.

1979-1982
UNITED JERSEY MIDSTATE

Employed at entry-level management trainee position, acquired experience in all banking areas. Analyzed financial statements, collateral
record posting, credit investigations, checking and savings account
maintenance, and beginning teller level one procedures.

In 1981 promoted to position of Supervising Teller. In that capacity
supervised office consisting of ten employees in all teller functions.

In addition, served as customer services representative with full responsibility for consumer loans, opening new accounts, branch audits,
and requisition of all supplies.

Resigned due to husband's transfer.

REFERENCES

On Request

Synopsis of Resume of: 82 Gifford St.
DOROTHY FERGUSON   Falmouth, MA 02540
                                                Phone: (617) 335-8720

OBJECTIVE

Nursing Assistant

EMPLOYMENT

1982-Present   NATIONAL HOME HEALTH CARE, Falmouth, MA.
                Major provider of health care services.
                    Nursing Assistant - certified; registered.

1973-1981   FALMOUTH PENNYSAVER, weekly newspaper
                    Typesetter; Compugraphic operator.

Prior   Stenographic, secretarial work (1950-60) at
                Columbia University, American Airlines, Kelly
                Girl. Homemaker (1960-1973).

EDUCATION

1947   High school diploma from Central High, Detroit, MI
                    Typing/shorthand award.
1950-1960   Columbia University, NYC
                    Liberal Arts courses.

Other: Vocational-Technical School, Boston, MA.
                    Nursing Assistant Certification.
1981-82   One-year course covered: patient personal care;
                taking vital signs; emergency techniques; feeding;
                CPR; psychology; general geriatric and patient care.

                Included nine weeks' hands-on hospital and nursing
                home training under supervision of two registered
                nurses. In addition, learned report writing, and noting
                detailed observation of patient's condition.

PERSONAL

Mature widow; three grown married children; good health.
Hobbies: reading; church choir and activities; music.
Affiliations: DAR; Girls' Club Auxilliary.

(FOR AMPLIFICATION SEE FOLLOWING)

Mature woman who has taken nursing training and changed careers in her later life.

Amplified Resume

Dorothy Ferguson
-page 2-

EMPLOYMENT HIGHLIGHTS

1982-Present
NATIONAL HOME HEALTH CARE

Upon certification, employed by firm that provides health care at all levels to medical facilities as well as to nursing homes and private homes.

Employed as "Nursing Assistant" on individual case basis, on hourly wage. Is called by firm, given detailed briefing on patient case history as well as level of care currently needed. Cases vary in length from a week to three months.

Cases handled have included: stroke victims, heart attack recovery, burn victims, and severe accident victims. When assigned case in a nursing home, is under the general supervision of home nursing supervisor.

Registers and shows certification upon arrival at home. Assumes assigned duties; makes detailed report of daily activities to supervisor and to firm at conclusion of on-duty period. Has earned excellent reputation for reliability and efficiency resulting in call-back requests from various area homes and a minimum of monitoring supervision.

When assigned to private home case assumes full responsibility for patient charge within the specific framework of given instructions. Can encompass bed-bath, bed-change, massage, back-rub, change of bandages, giving oxygen, and personal grooming. Carefully charts patient activity during duty: intake and output of food and liquid, skin tone, changes of mood or attitude, vital signs, general demeanor.

Has increased value as nursing assistant by painstaking attention to the credo "Know Your Limitation," while assuming those tasks which add to patient's morale and general well-being. Determines patient's interests and/or hobbies for interesting discussions when timely; reads to patients; writes letters and notes for those who cannot; encourages "walks" and "wheelchair rides" where permitted. Has received innumerable gifts and letters of appreciation from former patients and has never been asked to leave a case.

Reason for desiring change: Greater monetary compensation.

REFERENCES

Available

Synopsis of Resume of: 862 Rupert St.
RUTH ROGERS   McLean, VA 22101
                                                 Phone: (202) 632-9844

OBJECTIVE

General Duty Nursing

EXPERIENCE

1978-Present	Millville Veterans Hospital, Falls Church, VA '78-'80 - General Duty - Amputee Ward. '80- Charge Nurse - Paraplegic Ward.
1974-1978	Caldwell County Hospital, Alexandria, VA '74-'76 - Emergency Room Supervisor '76-'78 - Surgical Head Nurse
1970-1974	Mercy Hospital, Hornell, NY St. Mary's Hospital, Rochester, NY General duty nursing

EDUCATION

1966-1968	University of Michigan Liberal Arts
1968-1970	Hospital School of Nursing, Kalamazoo, MI R.N. Degree
Other:	State Board Examination: California, New York, Virginia
Current:	Courses in Geriatrics, Cardiac, Shock
Affiliations:	American Nurses Association Michigan State Nurse Association University Hospital Nurses Alumni Association

PERSONAL

Born:	1946. Health: excellent.
Hobbies:	Bridge; theater; tennis; golf.
Misc.	Have necessary clearance required for dispensing drugs.

(FOR AMPLIFICATION SEE FOLLOWING)

*An average record polished to appear brighter through emphasis on ability to cope
with change and scrupulously follow orders.*

Amplified Resume   Ruth Rogers
                                                    -page 2-

EXPERIENCE

1978-Present
Millville Veterans Hospital, Falls Church, VA

Accepted position in Amputee Ward after becoming familiar with the
facility due to terminal illness of veteran husband. In 1980, promoted to Charge Nurse in the Paraplegic Ward. Supervised all professional personnel assigned to the unit, including those in the
physical therapy area. Have found work satisfying and gratifying;
have established excellent relations with patients, subordinates,
and superiors; have been offered opportunity to raise present
classification.

Reason for desiring change: Death of husband and desire to affil-
iate with non-government facility.

1974-1978
Caldwell County Hospital, Alexandria, VA

After marriage relocated in Virginia and accepted temporary position
as staff nurse. In four months was offered, and accepted, position
as Emergency Room Supervisor. Filled in occasionally as Surgical
Head Nurse, and when vacancy occurred was offered permanent position
in that capacity.

Reason for leaving: Terminal illness of husband.

1970-1974
Mercy Hospital, St. Mary's Hospital, Hornell and Rochester, NY

As general duty staff nurse, supervised professional and non-profes-
sional workers assigned to work area; relieved Charge Nurse when
required. In general, made preliminary observations of patients'
conditions; prepared them for medical treatment. Took histories,
kept charts, assisted physicians with physical examinations and
treatments. In addition, prepared equipment for treatment and
tests; instructed patients in home care. Observed symptoms; noted
case progress as well as results of medical and nursing treatment.
Attended personal needs of patients; administered special diets,
medicines and treatment as prescribed. Assisted physicians with
treatments, dressings, and examination preparation. Kept records
of narcotics and other drugs signed out; received special recognition for detecting irregularities in records.

Reason for leaving: To get married.

REFERENCES

On request

Synopsis of Resume of:
WARNER WALKER

553 Couch St.
Portland, OR 97209
Phone: (503) 229-9050

JOB OBJECTIVE

Position in two- to three-doctor office, utilizing paramedic
training and experience

EXPERIENCE

1983-Present	SOUTH COUNTY FIRE DEPARTMENT, Portland, OR Journeyman Fire Fighter/Paramedic
1977-1983	LANTERN ELECTRIC CO., Portland, OR Estimator-bidder - promoted from electrician's helper
1976-1977	RAYBRO ELECTRIC CO., Baker, OR From stock clerk to front office

EDUCATION

Baker High School, Baker, OR. Graduated.

Other.
Part-time vocational school. Evening courses.
Emergency Medical Tech. Course I - 200 hours.
Emergency Medical Tech. Course II - 500 hours.

LICENSES

Fixed Wing and Helicopter pilot's license.

PERSONAL

Age: 32
Hobbies:
Affiliations:
Married, two children; health--excellent.
Flying; scuba diving; snow skiing; chess.
State Fire Fighters Association.

(FOR AMPLIFICATION SEE FOLLOWING)

*Comparatively new field. Thrust of resume is on his hard-core experience in the
paramedic field, as well as temperament —important in a field requiring cool head in
emergency.*

Amplified Resume   Warner Walker
                                                    -page 2-

PARAMEDIC EXPERIENCE

1983-Present
SOUTH COUNTY FIRE DEPARTMENT (Combined Fire and Ambulance Rescue Service)

Accepted in department after careful screening and background check
as to morals, temperament, ability to live in close quarters,
physical stamina, emotional stability, and genuine concern for
people.

Completed necessary courses for state certification in fire fighting; promoted through ranks to present status of Journeyman Fire
Fighter.

Due to unique operation combining fire and ambulance services, fire-
men are encouraged to take free medical technician training made
available at local vocational school and hospitals.

Took and passed Emergency Medical Technician's Course I, which
stresses: emergency care, maintenance of airway, control of bleed-
ing, shock management, emergency baby delivery, and basic life support.

Continued through EMT-II to become fully qualified Paramedic. At
this level "scene evaluation" is added, along with cardiopulmonary
resuscitation, intubation, defibrillation, IVs, and drugs, as well
as advanced life support.

As a Paramedic is permitted to work on own responsibility following
strict protocol, through IVs to defibrillation if warranted. Calls
hospital, acts as "doctor's long arm," meticulously following physician's phone instructions until patient's removal to the hospital.

Works 24-hour shift, followed by 48-hour off duty. During duty
hours teaches basic first aid to fire fighter apprentices, in addition to standard fire fighting duties and ambulance response.

Reason for desiring change: Although twice cited for fire fighting
action, feels that, by temperament, is better suited to paramedic
aspect of job in which he excels. Would prefer position with small
staff of private doctors who could utilize his training and practical know-how in their work.

REFERENCES

On request

Resume of: 9009 Fox St.
CHERYL LARSON   Denver, CO 80204
                                                 Phone: (303) 874-7588

JOB OBJECTIVE

Position in Cardiopulmonary Department. Flexible, willing to learn
through new experiences and advanced studies in present or related
fields.

EDUCATION

1983-1985   Hillsview Junior College, Colorado Springs, CO
                   Assoc. degree in Respiratory Therapy
                 Courses included:
                   Airway Management, Artificial Ventilation Therapy,
                   Cardiopulmonary Resuscitation, Chest Physiotherapy,
                   General Patient Care.

1985-Present   St. Joseph Hospital, Denver, CO
                   Classroom and laboratory training augmented with
                   hospital orientation. Started as Respiratory Therapy
                   Technician Trainee, in work-job program.

EMPLOYMENT

1985-Present   St. Joseph Hospital (same as above)
                   Employed part-time as Respiratory Therapy Techni-
                   cian III.

                 Performs respiratory therapy and EKG duties: venti-
                   lator installation, blood tests, pulmonary function
                   studies, breathing treatments.

                 Active on "Code Blue" team. Gives outpatient instruc-
                   tion on proper breathing techniques; attends emer-
                   gency pacemaker placement; assists in stress testing
                   and holter-monitor fitting.

PERSONAL

Age: 23   Single. Health: excellent.
Hobbies: Skiing; biking; hiking; camping; aerobics.
Affiliations: Denver Ski Club; Young Republicans.

REFERENCES

On request

*Student record with limited employment and good training, has more punch by
deleting synopsis.*

Synopsis of Resume of: 603 Murray St.
DOROTHY L. HOPKINS   Little Rock, AR 72219
                                          Phone: (501) 371-1832

JOB OBJECTIVE

Dental Hygienist in Periodontal Field

EDUCATION

1975   University of Tennessee, Memphis, TN
              College of Denistry - School of Dental Hygiene.
              Graduated.

Other: Hendrix College, Conway, AK. Graduated 1957.

              Continuing workshops in special areas to fulfill require-
              ments of dental hygienist license renewal.

EMPLOYMENT

1976-Present George A. Johnson, D.D.S. - Periodontist.
              900 W. Markan St., Little Rock, AK.
                Dental Hygienist in office with four full-time and
                three part-time employees.

1975-1976   Wallace Fowler, D.D.S. - General Practice.
                Dental Hygienist.

PERSONAL

Born: 1945. Married; children self-supporting.
Health: Excellent.
Hobbies: Gardening; tennis; home do-it-yourself projects.
Affiliations: American Dental Hygiene Society.

(FOR AMPLIFICATION PLEASE SEE FOLLOWING)

*Better than average education in her field, thus it appears ahead of employment.
Amplification stresses experience and dependability.*

Amplified Resume   Dorothy L. Hopkins
                                                  -page 2-

EXPERIENCE

1976-Present
GEO. A. JOHNSON, D.D.S. - PERIODONTIST

   As highly skilled, experienced hygienist in the office of one of the
area's leading periodontists, has myriad duties of specialized
nature performed without supervision.

   Performs oral prophylaxis, as well as some root planing and curret-
tage. Places and removes periodontal dressings; gives postoperative
instructions. Takes blood pressure readings; takes and develops
X-rays.

   Charts mouths; does cavity and oral cancer surveys. Does fluoride
treatments; takes patient histories.

   Percentage of time is devoted to patient education. Involves:
staining teeth to reveal plaque; pointing out presence of plaque;
emphasizing and demonstrating proper brushing and flossing tech-
niques and importance of regular home care.

Reason for change:
Dr. Johnson is retiring. He may be contacted for reference. His
letter of reference states in part, "Mrs. Hopkins is my dependable
right arm; my patients love her."

1975-1976
WALLACE FOWLER, D.D.S. - General Practice

   Accepted position as dental hygienist performing standard functions;
prophylaxis; charted patient's mouths; did cavity surveys; took and
developed X-rays; confirmed and made appointments.

   Left to accept position in preferred periodontal field.

REFERENCES

On request

Synopsis of Resume of:
ROSEMARY LONDON

998 Chapel St.
New Haven, CT 06510
Phone: (203) 927-5771

JOB OBJECTIVE

Position as Medical Assistant, 30-35 hours per week, preferably with regular hours and schedule important for diabetic management.

EDUCATION

1985   Whittier Vocational School, New Haven, CT
          Medical Assistant Program encompassing:
        Administrative
          Scheduling and receiving patients; obtaining patients' data; maintaining medical records; typing and medical transcription; handling phones and correspondence; office care, management, insurance matters, accounts, collection.
        Clinical
          Preparing patients for examination; obtaining vital signs; taking medical histories; assisting with treatments; performing routine office lab procedures and electrocardiograms; sterilizing instruments and equipment; instructing patients in preparation for X-ray and tests.

Other: Community College, Glenside, PA
           Business courses.

Special Skills
Typing, medical transcribing Peg Board, routine bookkeeping, billing, collections, interviewing, CPR, EKG, Aseptic Technique, Venipuncture, Finger Stick, Injections, Basic Laboratory.

Special Knowledge
Diabetes Mellitus and Insulin. Lectured in field for Medical Assistant Program. Invited back as guest lecturer for future classes. Circumstances permitting, desires to become active in instruction of diabetics as part of, or in addition to, medical assistant duties.

Certification
National Certification Examination. American Association of Medical Assistants.

PERSONAL

Born 1942; health - excellent, Diabetes Mellitus, Class I. Single, one self-supporting son; owns home, car; will travel and relocate.

(FOR AMPLIFICATION SEE FOLLOWING)

Example of physical problem which must be acknowledged but not dwelled upon, with emphasis on current and transferrable skills in new field. Does not lend itself to standard synopsis format.

Amplified Resume   Rosemary London
                                                    -page 2-

EMPLOYMENT CHRONOLOGY

1963-1965
CONNECTICUT GENERAL LIFE INSURANCE CO.

> Employed initially as group insurance contract analyst. Promoted
> to Production Supervisor, Group Insurance Underwriting which en-
> compassed training and lecturing as well as setting up and conduct-
> ing workshops. Left for marriage.

1968-1970

> Returned as assistant to personnel manager. Screened and inter-
> viewed job applicants; took dictation as well as handling corre-
> spondence on own; supervised payroll. Left to spend more time with
> young son.

1970-1985
COMMUNITY INVOLVEMENT

> As member of League of Women Voters, used writing, research, and
> editorial skills for brochures and press releases. Also lectured
> and assisted in formation of speakers' bureau.

> Named Concert Chairman of Community Concert Association, was respon-
> sible for all local arrangements for visiting artists (transporta-
> tion and accommodations), staging, and union liaison.

> Researched dietetic nutrition, organized support group for exchange
> of information.

GENERAL

> With son no longer dependent, desires to enter new field, fully
> utilizing former solid experience and newly acquired education and
> skills. Member American Association of Medical Assistants, and
> American Diabetes Association.

REFERENCES

On request

Synopsis of Resume of:
HARRY KRAMER

12 Shoreham Park
Denver, CO 80290
Phone: (303) 297-4292

JOB OBJECTIVE

Overall Restaurant Management (Food and Beverage)

EMPLOYMENT

1978-Present: ASSISTANT CHEF (20 kitchen personnel)
White Horse Motor Inn and Restaurant
Mountain View Rd., Denver, CO

1974-1978 MANAGER FOOD PREPARATION FOR COLLEGE STUDENTS
Westover College, Sundale, MI
(Employed by Corbett Co., 60 Fisher Bldg. Detroit, MI)

1972-1974 CHIEF STEWARD
Detroit German Club, Stillson St., Detroit, MI

1971-1972 CHEF (Heavy food preparation - no short orders)
Golden Diner, 1700 Main St., Detroit, MI

1970-1971 SUPERVISING CHEF (party and volume luncheon business)
Hilltop Restaurant, Broad St., Detroit, MI

TRAINING

1965-1970 Presbyterian College of North Carolina.
Business Administration.
Hofbrau Hotel, Stuttgart, Germany.
Three-year apprenticeship

PERSONAL

Born: 1947. Excellent health. Free to relocate.
Hobbies: Music; travel; painting.

(FOR AMPLIFICATION SEE FOLLOWING)

*Only principal jobs are listed to spotlight skills and wide range of experience. Interim
jobs were of lesser importance and to list them would serve no real purpose.
"General" sums up overall record, which will be discussed in full at interview.*

Amplified Resume   Harry Kramer
                                                        -page 2-

EMPLOYMENT HIGHLIGHTS

1978-Present
WHITE HORSE MOTOR INN AND RESTAURANT
(Serves 1,500 meals per day with varied menus;
single breakfasts to large banquets)

    Employed as Assistant Chef. Supervises overall operation of the
kitchen in normal operation. Lays out daily work schedules for 20
personnel; personally prepares all sauces and specialized European
dishes for this quality restaurant (considered to be one of the top
restaurants in Denver and surrounding area).

    In spite of insistence on discipline and refusal to settle for less
than best efforts, personnel turnover has been lower than average
for restaurants of similar class. Personal record is such, present
employer may be contacted for reference.

    Reason for desiring change: To move up to top position.

1974-1978
CORBETT COMPANY

    Employed by Corbett Co. (contractors for cafeteria and restaurant
operation) to manage the student feeding operation at Westover College, located in the suburbs of Lansing, Michigan. Planned and
scheduled menus; purchased all supplies; hired and trained necessary
personnel (usually students - consequently required manipulation of
manpower schedules to fit class schedules). In addition, kept all
records and did own bookkeeping.

    Paid per student rate by college, but operated on a cost-plus basis
rebating difference (if any) to the school. Restaurant so well operated alumni dinners were held there for the first time. This
allowed extra profit, with the end result that refunds were made
to the college every month of operation; reached maximum of $4,000
for a single month.

    Record resulted in transfer to Detroit into the Auto Dealers Insti-
tute. Proved to be industrial type cafeteria operation, utilizing
but small portion of his extensive training and skill.

    Reason for leaving: Resigned to seek more suitable post.

1972-1974
DETROIT GERMAN CLUB

    Employed as Chief Steward in charge of all restaurant activity in-
cluding purchasing. Developed steady banquet and special dinner
business which returned substantial profit to club and paid for
extensive club improvements. Left for better position.

References on request

Synopsis of Resume of: 453 Woodland Rd., Apt. #5
MARK J. SANDERSON   Grand Rapids, MI 49509
                                          Phone: (616) 530-7350

OBJECTIVE

Position of responsibility and growth potential in hotel field

EMPLOYMENT

1978-Present   MERRMAC HOTELS, Grand Rapids, MI
                540 rooms; 8 restaurants, lounges, and bars.
                    Manager Guest Services - steady climb from desk
                    clerk.

EDUCATION

1976-1978   Grand Valley State Colleges, Allendale, MI
                    Degree: B.S. in Hospitality & Tourism; minor -
                    Social Science; average: 3.9.
                    A c t i v i t i e s:
                    Dean's Advisory Council; Residence Hall Advisor.
                    H o n o r s:
                    Phi Kappa Phi; International Study Scholarship;
                    Honor Scholarship; Presidential Scholarship Final-
                    ist.

1974-1976   North Central Michigan College, Petoskey, MI
                    Liberal Arts; transferred to above.

Expenses: Miscellaneous part-time employments to help defray costs:
                teaching assistant and tutor; audit clerk; lodge desk
                clerk.

PERSONAL

Age: 26   Married; excellent health; free to relocate.
Hobbies: Backgammon; furniture refinishing; antiques; cooking.

(FOR AMPLIFICATION SEE FOLLOWING)

Resume technique shows progression in one-job employment history.

Amplified Resume   Mark J. Sanderson
                                                        -page 2-

EMPLOYMENT CHRONOLOGY

1978-Present
MERRMAC HOTELS

1978
Hired initially as desk clerk with following responsibilities: regis-
tering all hotel guests; posting charges to guest accounts; room
assignments; assisting in making future room reservations. Bonded as
cashier; required knowledge of computer system and maintenance of computer records.

1980
Promoted to Night Clerk/Auditor. Principal responsibilities: maintenance of computer system; auditing of cashier and bank reports; re-
solving guests' complaints; supervision of staff of five; generating
statistics and information regarding daily sales for distribution to
General Manager and miscellaneous executives.

1984
Promoted to Guest Services Manager with supervisory responsibility for
48 employees.

Areas of supervision include: bell stand, valet parking, special guest
services. Initiated new management style, establishing employee task
force to discuss problems and grievances for ultimate solution by
mutual agreement.

Keeps in constant daily touch with "line employees"; initiates training
programs where need is indicated; solicits feedback on policies; re-
views employee performance on regular basis, issuing evaluation reports
to management.

Among responsibilities, oversees details of celebrated VIP guest arrangements: meeting, greeting, newspaper releases, special menus,
beverages, floral arrangements, and special services.

Reason for desiring change:

Career move to larger market.

REFERENCES

On Request. Please do not contact present employer
until after interview.

Synopsis of Resume of: 843 Oakland Beach
JENNY MARKS   Rye, NY 10580
                                          Phone: (914) 849-9906

OBJECTIVE

Executive or Legal Secretary

EMPLOYMENT

1981-Present   AMALGAMATED PRODUCTIONS, INC., New York, NY
                Motion Pictures and Television Production
                Administrative Assistant to President.

1978-1981   NDA Broadcasting, 51 West 62nd St., New York, NY
                Executive Secretary to Vice President, Business
                Affairs.

1975-1978   AMERICAN BRANDS, INC., 245 Park Ave., New York, NY
                Administrative Assistant - Legal Dept.

1970-1975   POTOMAC SCHOOL, McLean, VA
                Business Practice Teacher.

Other: Miscellaneous vacation jobs to help defray college ex-
                penses: legal stenographer, courthouse clerk, resort
                desk clerk, tour guide.

EDUCATION

1969   Western Michigan University, Kalamazoo, MI
                B.S. in Political Science; minor - business.
                Dean's List all four years.

Other: Special courses in speed reading and writing; paralegal
                seminars.

Skills: Typing; shorthand; calculator; word processor; computer;
                speech writing; editing.

PERSONAL

Born 1948 in Park Ridge, Illinois; single; free to travel and relocate.
Hobbies: Competition ballroom dancing (has won several trophies); fitness classes; reading; French cooking; duplicate bridge.

(FOR AMPLIFICATION SEE FOLLOWING)

Amplified Resume

Jenny Marks
-page 2-

EMPLOYMENT HIGHLIGHTS

<u>1981-Present</u>
<u>AMALGAMATED PRODUCTIONS, INC.</u>

Hired as "Girl Friday" at this new firm. Set up and organized office; purchased office supplies, machines, and filing cabinets; set up system. Promoted to Assistant to the Story Editor after one year with substantial increase in salary and responsibilities.

Did "first reading" of scripts; participated in story conferences, made recommendations as to final selections; assisted in editing and proofing finished products. In 1983 made Administrative Assistant to the President, handled all correspondence; prepared status and expense reports; approved bills and initiated payments according to contracts.

In addition, made all travel arrangements; screened calls; operated on own assuming all responsibilities in frequent absence of the president. Made decisions and given free rein to exercise own judgment in many critical areas.

<u>Reason for leaving</u>: Would like to return to private sector.

<u>1978-1981</u>
<u>NDA BROADCASTING</u>

In capacity as executive secretary to vice president in charge of business affairs, prepared and issued contracts and payment authorizations for talent and staff involved in TV productions. Handled all details of producers' expenses; approved bills and prepared expense reports. Left to accept better position with more potential above.

<u>1975-1978</u>
<u>AMERICAN BRANDS, INC.</u>

As administrative assistant in Legal Department, had full responsibility for myriad financial transactions and paperwork inherent in the position. Worked closely with bank employees, sales representatives, and general public. Left to enter media field.

<u>1970-1975</u>
Upon graduation from college, accepted interim teaching position in metropolitan area in order to become oriented to larger markets. Enjoyed public contact with students, parents, administrators, and community as well as responsibilities. Left for position in New York City.

REFERENCES

On request

Synopsis of Resume of: 45 Barnes Ave.
PETER DIXON   Memphis, TN 38118
                                                Phone: (901) 863-2819

JOB OBJECTIVE

Purchasing Agent or position leading to it in near future

EMPLOYMENT

1978-Present   NATIONAL DYNAMICS CORPORATION
                    1800 Cruger Ave., Memphis, TN
                    Buyer - Mechanical Components

1975-1978   LEWIN MANUFACTURING CO. (Office furniture & supplies)
                    1328 Taft Ave., Atlanta, GA
                    General Purchasing Agent

1970-1975   SCHULTZ FABRICATORS (Plastic fabricators)
                    East Atlanta, GA
                    Purchasing Agent

1966-1970   WHITE CO., INC. (Hospital equipment manufacturers)
                    Nashville, TN
                    Metals Buyer

EDUCATION

                    Brothers Institute, Indianapolis, IN. Graduated 1966.

Evening School: Jefferson Institute, Indianapolis, IN. Machine Shop
                        course
                    Alva Technical School, Nashville, TN. Chemistry
                        (one-year course).
                    Atlanta Institute of Technology. Industrial Mgmt.
                        course.
                    Memphis Tech. Metallurgy (one-year course).

PERSONAL

Born: 5/30/48; married; three children; health good.
Hobbies: Sports (spectator and participation); duplicate bridge.
Affiliations: American Society for Metals.

(FOR AMPLIFICATION SEE FOLLOWING)

*Type of material purchased is mentioned, as well as approximate size of company, to
show applicant's level of purchase responsibility. Yearly income (despite increases) in
low bracket, therefore mention of it is avoided.*

Amplified Resume   Peter Dixon
                                                    -page 2-

                        EMPLOYMENT HIGHLIGHTS

1978-Present
NATIONAL DYNAMICS CORPORATION (approx. 2,000 employees)

    Employed as Buyer of Mechanical Components in the Electronics Divi-
    sion, with two expediters under his direction. Operates on own
    responsibility, locates suppliers, issues orders without supervision.
    Nearly all work in the division is on government contract with time
    and quality paramount; consequently, his object is to obtain mater-
    ials consistently up to specifications from firms who can be depen-
    ded upon for delivery.

    Travels to vendors' plants throughout the United States checking
    facilities; keeps records which are referred to when placing orders.
    Reads blueprints; interprets production orders to insure delivery of
    materials in proper sequence, avoiding production delay.

    Purchases such materials as: panels, springs, hinges, chassis,
    metal cabinets. Familiar with metals and plastics, and accustomed
    to ordering to extremely close tolerances. Replaced two buyers
    (metal components and hardware) and has done the work of both.

    Results:
    Consistently received proper material with very low percentage of
    rejects. Ten buyers were recommended for salary increases at last
    evaluation period; was one of two selected for the increase. Yearly
    income has risen by $5,850 since start.

    Reason for change: To improve status.

1975-1978
LEWIN MANUFACTURING COMPANY (approx. 700 employees)

    As General Purchasing Agent was responsible for four buyers and en-
    tire purchase activity. Purchases were in substantial seven figures,
    from vendors in southern and midwestern U.S.

    Reason for leaving: Was given no authority to run his department.
    Held responsible for acts of subordinates, but could not enforce his
    orders to them. Resigned when situation became intolerable.

1970-1975
SCHULTZ FABRICATORS (approx. 300 employees)

    General Purchasing Agent, also in charge of inventory control.
    Record was such was approached by above firm and offered better pay-
    ing, more responsible position above.

                        References available

Synopsis of Resume of: 305 Smull Ave.
JEANNETTE McDONOUGH   North Caldwell, NJ 07006
                                                (212) 943-9876

OBJECTIVE

Administrative Secretary or Assistant

EXPERIENCE

1979-Present   CALDWELL COUNTY SCHOOL SYSTEM, North Caldwell, NJ
& 1977-1978   Administrative Secretary

1978-1979   ATWATER COUNTY SCHOOL SYSTEM, Columbus, OH
                    Administrative Secretary

1975-1977   MALCOME & WRIGLEY - law firm, Columbus, OH
                    Legal Secretary
                    Resigned to move out of state.

Prior   Fashion-Rite Blouse Manufacturing, Peru, IN.
                    Began as apprentice out of high school. Intensive,
                    overall training in: ordering supplies, shipments,
                    handling piecework payroll for over 200 employees,
                    preparing P.&L. statements, income taxes. Assistant
                    to General Manager when resigned for marriage.

EDUCATION

Bunkerhill High School, Bunkerhill, IN
    Commercial Diploma.
Course in CPT word-processing computerized equipment.

Skills

Typing; manual shorthand; dictating machine; word processor.

Personal

Born: 1941; one dependent child; excellent health; will re-
                locate.

Hobbies: Physical fitness; crafts; music.

Affiliations: Women's Network (corresponding secretary); church organ-
                ist and choir director; Boy Scout Parent Support
                Group.

(FOR AMPLIFICATION SEE FOLLOWING)

Employing chronology to clarify and highlight solid, somewhat fragmented
experience.

Amplified Resume

Jeannette McDonough
-page 2-

EMPLOYMENT HIGHLIGHTS

COUNTY SCHOOL SYSTEMS CHRONOLOGY

1977-1978
Employed in Caldwell County School System as administrative secretary to the Director of Language Arts and Data Processing with standard secretarial duties. Was recommended for promotion to Superintendent's office when family illness necessitated return to Ohio.

1978-1979
Accepted temporary position as Administrative Secretary to Superintendent of Schools in Columbus, Ohio. Screened phone calls, handled all business and composed personal correspondence. Made travel arrangements; prepared agenda for school board and cabinet meetings. Resigned to return to New Jersey.

1979-Present
Re-employed in dual capacity as administrative secretary to the Superintendent of Caldwell County schools, as well as the five-member school board.
Superintendent responsibilities include: making appointments, taking dictation for all business and personal correspondence; travel arrangements; expense accounts; issuing vouchers; channeling mail for school system; general supervision of clerical personnel.

School board responsibilities: travel arrangements; expenses; special notices and correspondence. Prepares agenda for weekly school board meetings; supervises collating 200-300 packets for distribution to 95 members of school system.

Sets up time and location for board meetings; attends meeting and makes summary of tape-recorded minutes for distribution at next board meeting. Meets with press personally and on phone to clarify results of weekly meetings as to agenda resolution.

Overall duties include: office purchases, budget preparation for school board, school attorney, and Superintendent.

Took special training in word-processing computerized equipment installed two years ago. Is entirely comfortable with the system and has recommended an increase in number of stations for clerical personnel.

Has had across-the-board salary increases yearly as determined by outcome of union/administration negotiations. Request to be put on administrative salary scale pending.

Reason for desiring change: Salary commensurate with responsibilities.

References on request

Synopsis of Resume of: 87 Kenwood Ave.
BRUCE R. SHEAHAN   New Orleans, LA 70150
                                          Phone: (504) 239-1063

JOB OBJECTIVE

Position in Customer Service or Sales Field

EMPLOYMENT

1983-Present   MANAGER MARKETING ADMINISTRATION
                Apex Equipment Sales, Inc., New Orleans, LA

1979-1983   CUSTOMER SERVICE MAN
                Altex Fixture, Inc., Baton Rouge, LA

1976-1979   SALESPERSON
                Morris Sales and Service Co., Hot Springs, AR

1972-1976   SALESPERSON
                Brock-Hall Food Co., Hot Springs, AR
                Route salesperson: resigned to accept better position.

EDUCATION

College: Little Rock University, Little Rock, AR
                    Evening School, 1972-1976.
                    Business Administration course of study
Other: Company-sponsored sales training courses
                Correspondence course in Accounting (current)

PERSONAL

Born: 6/11/53: married; three children; health--excellent.
Affiliations: Sales Executives Club of New Orleans; Rotary Interna-
                tional.

(FOR AMPLIFICATION SEE FOLLOWING)

*Qualifications for present job objective given focus by position titles on synopsis
sheet, and credibility is indicated through amplified details.*

Amplified Resume   Bruce R. Sheahan
                                                        -page 2-

EMPLOYMENT HIGHLIGHTS

1983-Present
APEX EQUIPMENT SALES, INC.
(Manufacturers dental, surgical, laboratory equipment)

Employed originally to assist the manager of dental equipment sales
section, as well as replace him during yearly monthly vacations and
regular trip absences.

Handled all customer correspondence, all inside customer contact by
phone or plant visitation. Had all dental equipment orders properly
entered and routed through plant. Maintained regular contact with
twenty-five representatives throughout the southwest.

Retained position throughout transition period following sale of
company to present owners. Promoted to newly created position of
Manager of Marketing Administration supervising eight personnel in
processing all orders entering plant for all products. Yearly dollar volume: low eight figures.

Handled all customer correspondence; revised order handling procedure, resulting in substantial reduction in order handling costs.

Reason for leaving: New ownership resulted in frequent policy and
personnel changes, creating atmosphere of impermanence. Recent promotion added responsibility with no monetary increase. Submitted
resignation. Has agreed to remain for short period (not exceeding
three months) to assist in training replacement. Currently available
for interview.

1979-1983
ALTEX FIXTURE, INC.
(Wood and plastic display equipment)

Employed as Sales Trainee and Apprentice to Sales Engineer. Moved
directly into customer sales department with full charge of all order
details on repair of returned or defective goods and parts replacement. Remained in same capacity throughout employment, and was retained despite drastic cut in company sales force. Left for better
position.

1976-1979
MORRIS SALES AND SERVICE CO.
(Distributors offset and letterpress machines and equipment)

Employed as salesperson to cover six-county area. Earned reasonably
good commission income; however, repeat sales in long-life duplica-
ting machine category unlikely. Resigned to seek better opportunity.

References on request

Resume of: 752 Sherwood Ave.
ANDREA CUMMINGS   Sharon, CT 06069
                                              Phone: (203) 643-7792

JOB OBJECTIVE

Position in Sales and/or Demonstrating.

EMPLOYMENT

10/83-4/85
Demonstrator
Ward Baking Company
29 Clincon Ave., Sharon, CT

Employed as one of four in area to demonstrate and promote sale of special bakery items (for example, bake-and-serve-type rolls), as well as standard production items (bread, pastries, etc.).

With special equipment (oven, etc.), was transported to store selected for day's effort. Stores were located in small towns surrounding the Sharon, CT, area; were of varying size and type, consequently had widely varying clientele.

At demonstration worked alone, personally baking most items and offering samples to customers. After samples were consumed, solicited opinions on items, and suggested purchase of them. Was expected to sell stock of merchandise which accompanied demonstration, and at same time make an impression that would reflect favorably on company and store.

Results

1. Gave full employer-satisfaction. Maintained good volume of merchandise sale where possible (on occasion, store did so little business there were no customers to approach).

2. Gained valuable experience in courteously dealing with persons of all nationalities, age groups, and walks of life. Became knowledgeable in evaluating and handling prospects.

Reason for leaving: Involved in automobile accident; was replaced, of necessity, during convalescence.

(FOR AMPLIFICATION SEE FOLLOWING)

Minor level responsibility employment given added stature through major detail. Lack of formal education deemphasized through generalization of educational detail.

EMPLOYMENT
(continued)

10/80-9/83
Waitress

    Old Spain Restaurant, Sharon, CT. Quality restaurant catering to women's luncheon trade. Gained experience in meeting and dealing with public as well as handling money and coping with various problems posed by diners. Left to accept better position with Ward.

1/77-10/80
Salesclerk

    Hendricks (stationery store), Bridgeport, CT. Employed as temporary clerk during special promotion; record was such offered and accepted permanent position.

    Began in card and stationery department. Promoted to office equipment department, selling such costly equipment as desks, files, etc. Had regular contact with business and executive personnel; required good knowledge of items offered as well as proper technique to consummate sale. Left when family moved.

1976-1977
Part-time sales

    Various part-time salesclerk positions during high school period. Sold: houseware items, women's dresses, garden supplies

EDUCATION

Formal
    Bridgeport, CT, public schools.
Special Training
    Demonstration Training Course given by Ward Baking Co. General training in all phases of store operation gained in multiple store employment.

Note: Would enter training program if requisite to employment.

PERSONAL

Born: 9/2/58 in Bridgeport, CT. Marital status: single.
Health: Excellent.
Hobbies: Dancing; cooking.
General: Speaks with authority in well-modulated tones; good presence and command of English

(All former employers may be contacted for reference)

Synopsis of Resume of:
ROBERT E. SANDERSON

69 Canterbury Rd.
Corning, NY 14820
Phone: (716) 897-4676

JOB OBJECTIVE

Position in field of Marketing or Sales Supervision

EMPLOYMENT

1982-6/85	EASTERN SALES MANAGER Boyden Equipment Co., 80 Broad St., Chicago, IL
2/74-1982	ASSISTANT TO GENERAL SALES MANAGER (Moved up from trainee through Sales Staff Group) Scovell-Hill, Inc., Schenectady, NY
1971-1974	ASSISTANT TO PRESIDENT, Consultant-- Morgan Machine Tool Co., Universal Sports Car Sales, Foley Farm Equipment Co., Rochester, NY
Prior	Self-employed, owner-manager of appliance company, Buffalo, NY

EDUCATION

1960-1964	Niagara University, Niagara, NY B.S. in M.E.

Other:	University of Buffalo, evening school
	    Courses in science.
	U.S. Navy courses in:
	    Industrial Management, Strategy and Tactics, Logistics.

SERVICE

1964-1966	U.S. Navy. Completed N.R.O.T.C. in college. Currently holds rank of Commander in Reserve; is not required to participate in active duty.

PERSONAL

Born:	6/18/41. Married; two children. Health--excellent.
Residence:	Owns home; willing to relocate for proper opportunity.
Affiliations:	Toastmasters' Club; Rotary; active in politics.

(FOR AMPLIFICATION SEE FOLLOWING)

*Classic responsibility-result record, reflecting able man quickly taking situation in
hand, assuming additional responsibilities, with corresponding accomplishment.*

Amplified Resume

Robert E. Sanderson
-page 2-

EMPLOYMENT HIGHLIGHTS

1982-1985
BOYDEN EQUIPMENT COMPANY
(Manufacturers bulk milk cooling equipment)

Employed to direct company's sales effort in an area encompassing: New York State, Vermont, Connecticut, New Hampshire, and Maine. In Canada: Ontario, Quebec, and the Maritime Provinces.

Equipment is sold for use on individual dairy farms to store and cool milk prior to its collection. Sales are channeled through direct salespeople, manufacturers' representatives, distributors, dealers, and direct major accounts. These include Agway, United Cooperatives of Quebec, and other cooperatives or marketing groups who buy for members. Competition is intense, with over 50 competitive firms in area.

Hires, trains, fires, directs salespeople; makes territorial changes. Selects distributors and dealers, recommends credit limit for final decision by Credit Department. Works with dealer and distributor personnel, as well as direct salespeople, to aid and stimulate sales effort.

Results

1) Tripled an original dollar sales volume of low six figures.
2) Increased major direct cooperative accts. from four to ten.
3) Added nine key area distributors, plus seven key dealers.
4) Achieved effective distribution in all Canadian areas.
5) Company valuation of services indicated by an increase of $7,000 on a substantial starting yearly income.

Reason for change: Employed with understanding would become General Manager of company within short period. Recent change in company ownership makes appointment and/or further progress with company unlikely. Resigned.

REFERENCES

Available

Synopsis of Resume of:
SANDRA RICH-CARHART

410 Younger Rd.
Sarver, PA 16055
Phone: (412) 933-8740

JOB OBJECTIVE

Key position in sales capacity where achievement and communication skills will lead to enhanced opportunities and advancement.

EMPLOYMENT

<u>1983-Present</u>   CHLORINATOR REPLACEMENT PARTS, INC., Pittsburgh, PA
Manufacturer and sales representative

1981-1983   AMERICAN TELEPHONE CO., Syracuse, NY
Long Distance Service, Sales Representative

1980-1981   WORDFLOW SYSTEMS, INC. Syracuse, NY
Copiers. Service Representative

1975-1980   SYRACUSE GIRLS CLUB, Syracuse, NY
Program Aide. Developed recreational programs

Prior   Volunteer work while homemaker raising family:
Red Cross; hospital; PTA; teaching aide

EDUCATION

High School: Graduated 1968; worked summers as retail clerk.

Other: Sales seminars and workshops.

PERSONAL

Age: 38; single parent; teenage daughter semi-dependent. Excellent health. Hobbies: karate; jogging.

(FOR AMPLIFICATION SEE FOLLOWING)

Example of new breed of career woman in job market: the single parent, in the traveling sales field, formerly dominated by men.

Amplified Resume
Sandra Rich-Carhart
-page 2-

EMPLOYMENT HIGHLIGHTS

<u>1983-Present</u>
<u>CHLORINATOR REPLACEMENT PARTS, INC.</u>
Manufacturer, dealer, and distributor of parts used in equipment which
purifies drinking and waste water.

Employed by company to set up new sales division. Designed and wrote
promotional material and brochures. Researched state for prospective
customers.

Deals principally with municipalities, state institutions, and county
governments, as well as limited number of private companies. Requires
pioneer ground-breaking as well as making "cold calls" in areas to
determine persons in charge of ordering and purchase. Such persons can
range from city mayors to plant operators.

Has set up sales structure and weekly itinerary for smooth-running,
efficient operation. Sells parts; gives quotations; schedules repair
work.

Is on road approximately four days a week covering territory of approximately 3,000-mile radius. Has increased sales over 25% with no prior
experience with product.

<u>Reason for desiring change</u>: Upward career move where communication
skills could be more fully used.

<u>1981-1983</u>
<u>AMERICAN TELEPHONE COMPANY</u>

Employed as sales rep for this long-distance service company. Genera-
ted all leads; handled direct sales and customer relations. Was picked
by company to train new sales personnel; selected "Top Salesperson of
Year" in 1982. Left for better potential above.

<u>1980-1981</u>
<u>WORDFLOW SYSTEMS, INC.</u>

Employed as customer service representative making calls "cold" on potential customers to set up demonstrations of copier equipment. Worked
with customers to determine appropriate equipment needs. Dead end;
left for better position above.

REFERENCES

Available on request

Synopsis of Resume of: 418 West St.
FRED G. SNOW   Pittsburgh, PA 15235
                                          Phone: (412) 303-6224

JOB OBJECTIVE

Position in retail management field. Department store
or comparable operation.

EMPLOYMENT

1985-Present   MERCHANDISING MANAGER
                R.S. Wilson Department Store
                West Broadway, Pittsburgh, PA

1975-1985   STORE MANAGER (up through ranks from salesperson)
                Ward Roebuck & Co., NY
                Yearly income increased to $30,000 during employment

EDUCATION

High School: Lincoln High School, Providence, RI. Graduated.

1973-1975   Carnegie Business College, Pittsburgh, PA
                2-year course in Business Management included:
                Accounting, Auditing, Finance.

PERSONAL

Age: 35   Married, no children. Health--good.
Affiliations: American Legion; YMCA.
Hobbies: Painting; music; theater.

(FOR AMPLIFICATION SEE FOLLOWING)

*Salary mentioned in previous rather than present employment to alert prospective
employer to earning bracket without pinpointing amount. Strongly stated reason for
leaving present employment could be risky if previous employment record did not
indicate applicant's reliability.*

Amplified Resume   Fred G. Snow
                                                         -page 2-

EMPLOYMENT DETAILS

1985-Present
R.S. WILSON DEPARTMENT STORE

   Employed as Merchandise Manager with complete responsibility for
   all merchandising for entire store (composed of approximately 50
   depts.).

   Has situation well in hand and functioning smoothly; however, dis-
   agrees with company policies which he considers antiquated. Would
   make a change to a more aggressive company.

1975-1985
WARD ROEBUCK & COMPANY

   Originally employed as salesclerk in the Housewares Dept. of the
   company store in Providence, RI.

   Promoted in six months to Manager of the Mens' and Boys' Clothing
   Department.

   Promoted in one and one half years to Assistant Manager of a store
   with an operating personnel of 50.

   Promoted to Assistant Manager in Charge of Operations at the company's larger store in Boston, MA. Had charge of all operational
   functions.

   Promoted to Store Manager at Allentown, PA, a store with personnel
   of 35. After 18 months moved as Manager to a larger store (double
   the volume), at Scranton, PA. In 10 months increased volume by
   35% and was rated "Potential District Manager" material.

   In 1983 was promoted to Regional Merchandiser for 115 stores, with
   supervision of: (1) Women's Ready-to-Wear, (2) Domestic and Yard
   Goods, (3) Mens' and Boys' Hosiery, (4) Curtains and Drapes.

   In 1984 was moved to the large store in Baltimore, MD, as Manager.
   Store employed from 100 to 125 persons at various seasons. Managed
   store from June 1984 to April 1985. Despite national downward trend
   during that period, increased store's volume on a yearly basis over
   $550,000. Built an excellent record on turnover of personnel as
   well as housekeeping.

   Reason for leaving: Received what appeared to be an excellent offer
   from R.S. Wilson Dept. Store and, with the idea of broadening his
   experience, accepted.

REFERENCES AVAILABLE

Synopsis of Resume of: 987 Culver Ave.
DUDLEY M. HOWARD   Burlington, VT 05401
                                          Phone: (802) 749-9817

JOB OBJECTIVE

Position in Sales Management on District or Regional level

EMPLOYMENT

1985-Present   Haley Car Company, Burlington, VT
                    Appraiser and salesperson (interim work while seek-
                    ing suitable position)

1979-1985   Mansfield Motors, Rutland, VT
                    Sales Manager

1972-1976   Rutland Motor Sales, Rutland VT
                    Salesperson

1970-1972   Valley Cars, Inc. Shrewsburg, VT
                    Service Manager

1968-1970   Lakeport Marine Company, Lakeport, NH
                    Salesperson

EDUCATION

Formal: Rockland High School, Rockland, ME
                  State University of Maine, Orono, ME
                    Business Administration. Left voluntarily for
                    financial reasons. Activities: advertising manager
                    for college periodical.

Miscellaneous: Sales seminars and workshops

PERSONAL

Born: 1/15/46. Married; health--good.
Hobbies: Photography; amateur radio operator.

(FOR AMPLIFICATION SEE FOLLOWING)

*Pointing up qualities essential in all sales management: success in personal sales,
coupled with success in getting maximum sales effort when managing sales people.*

Amplified Resume   Dudley M. Howard
                                                      -page 2-

                        EMPLOYMENT HIGHLIGHTS

1985-Present
HALEY CAR COMPANY

   Appraiser and salesperson. Immediately sought and found position,
   not in line with personal experience and ability, but accepted on
   a temporary basis in preference to depriving family of income while
   seeking more suitable post. Present employer aware of circumstances,
   and may be contacted.

1979-1985
MANSFIELD MOTORS

   Employed as the second of four salespersons to revitalize sales in
   an agency in need of improved methods and sales. Sales rose sub-
   stantially in first year; was appointed Sales Manager.

   In this capacity, hired and trained five new salespersons. Set up
   a realistic sales program; instituted a bonus system to stimulate
   sales activity. In addition, established a follow-up program for
   sales team which operated as follows: each salesperson was required
   to call on each car purchaser one week after sale. Charged with the
   responsibility of checking on customer satisfaction, as well as to
   obtain names of friends who may have seen or ridden in the car, and
   could be logical prospects. A report on this call was mandatory,
   and proved valuable sales builder.

   Directed sales promotions, administration and advertising. Designed
   advertisements for local papers; developed special promotions. Conceived "Old Timers Parties" where special invitations were issued
   former customers (now on inactive list), special new car showing
   program arranged, refreshments served; results were excellent.

   Results:

   As Salesperson:
     Increased sales by 30% first year.

   As Sales Manager:
     Showed increases of over 35% each year. Increase from 14 cars per
     month in '80, to 50 on 1985. Agency rose from ninth to third in
     sales in the county.

   Reason for leaving: Friction developed between partner-owners, resulting in sale of interest to outsider who moved in new sales staff.
   Resigned in protest of what he felt to be unreasonable discharge of
   competent sales personnel.

              References available on request

Synopsis of Resume of:
HUGH STELJES

120 Farley St.
Indianapolis, IN 46241
Phone: (317) 611-9044

JOB OBJECTIVE

Position in drafting - Supervision - or leading to it

EMPLOYMENT

1/79-present	DRAFTSMAN I Electronic Communications, Inc. 200 Front St., Indianapolis, IN
1971-1979	School period employment (part-time and summers): Ace Vending Machine Co., Jefferson City, MO Employed by District Manager, repaired machines at home. Between school period employment (full-time): Miller Parts & Equipment Co., Jefferson City, MO Repaired heavy equipment (tractors, industrial equip., etc.) Offered substantial raise to remain; resigned to utilize education.

EDUCATION

1971-1975	Salem High School, Salem, MO
	Jefferson City High School, Jefferson City, MO
	  Took drafting; completed two years' credit in
	  Architectural Drafting.

1977-1979	Bates Technical Institute, Jefferson City, MO
	  Evening courses in: Basic Electronics,
	  Descriptive Geometry, Trigonometry, Drafting.

PERSONAL

Born:	1/21/54. Single. Health: good.
Hobbies	Music (plays piano); do-it-yourself repair projects.
Affiliations:	YMCA

(FOR AMPLIFICATION SEE FOLLOWING)

One-job background requiring thorough coverage to expose all capabilities.

EMPLOYMENT

1/79-Present
ELECTRONIC COMMUNICATIONS, INC.

Employed originally as Draftsman III. Learned company systems;
handled small detail drawings, electrical and mechanical.

In two years moved up to Class II. Prepared fabrication or detail
drawings required for manufacturing purposes. Worked with designers and engineers under minimum supervision. Also worked from engineering sketches, designs or layouts.

Was (and is) frequently given a rough sketch of a part or assembly
of parts with only main or overall dimensions specified. Required
to locate tubes, switches, other electronic or mechanical parts,
actually design package. Makes detail drawings of each element
using dimensions drawn from company tolerances and engineering
specifications, keeping whole package within overall dimensions
required.

Was selected for and assigned to a group of Design Engineers as
lead draftsman for specification control and procurement outline
drawings coverage on a multimillion dollar missile project. Required to be familiar with Ordnance and General Electric Corporation systems of drawing and procedures. Has at personal disposal,
and is familiar with, information on vendor items available for
purchase. Is authorized to select parts or units which fit overall
specifications. Is given almost full responsibility for this type
of mechanical item (frequently electronic or electrical).

Makes drawings of parts to be purchased; handles correspondence with
vendors. Also handles correspondence with Ordnance and Contract
Associates on matters pertaining to specifications. Has become
particularly expert in government procedures and specifications.

Promoted to Draftsman I during above assignment (was performing
duties associated with this classification from its inception). Is
now designing small units while continuing aforementioned responsibilities.

Reason for desiring change:

Better opportunity for advancement; more varied experience.

REFERENCES

Available

Resume of: 80 Brett St.
DAVID E. CLINTON   Seattle, WA 98101
                                    Phone: (206) 743-7635

OBJECTIVE

Position in field of Electronic Design or Drafting

EMPLOYMENT RECORD

1982-Present   ELECTRONIC DRAFTSMAN (Design)
                  Farrel Photo, Inc., Seattle, WA

1974-1982   Note:
                Jobs listed below are all project type; it is standard
                procedure for crews to be broken up upon successful com-
                pletion of project.

                DRAFTSMAN (electrical and mechanical)
                  National Electronics, Phoenix, AZ
                  Victor Design, Inc., Farmington, NM
                  Standard Products, Inc., Santa Barbara, CA
                  Morris Electronics, Los Angeles, CA
                  Milo Corp., Barstow, CA
                  Simco Electric Co., Tucson, AZ
                  Western Conductor Sales, Spokane, WA
                  Burns Electronics, Burns, OR

EDUCATION

Following high school graduation, has taken variety of
courses whenever time and employment permitted.
They include: Basic Engineering, Mechanical Drawing and
Engineering, Mathematics and Physics for Mechanical Engineering, Electronics.

PERSONAL

Born: 5/19/55. Health--Excellent. Single.
Residence: Rents; free to relocate; willing to travel; would accept
                overseas post.
Hobbies: Bowling; hunting; fishing.

(FOR AMPLIFICATION SEE FOLLOWING)

Demonstrating project or short-term employment technique, combining for clarity,
listing for credibility, giving logical reason for extraordinary number of job changes.

Amplified Resume   David E. Clinton
                                                    -page 2-

EMPLOYMENT HIGHLIGHTS

1982-Present

Farrel Photo, Inc. (350 employees)
Manufacturers photographic and microfilming apparatus.

Responsible for design, layout, and detailing of schematics and
wiring diagrams for various devices produced for U.S. Army and
U.S. Navy. Equipment is highly intricate; includes panel boards
providing selectivity in choice of film, number of duplications
and other variations, by push button. Contracts slated for completion; has been offered future assignment not in desired field;
declined.

Project Assignments: 1974-1981

National Electronics
Large manufacturer of electronic devices. Worked with company engineers and draftsmen in layout and design of classified equipment
to be used in the early warning and missile systems.

Victor Design, Inc.
Major manufacturer of air conditioning equipment. Did design and
layout of electrical wiring for commercial production.

Standard Products, Inc.
Manufacturer heavy-duty machine tools. Assisted in mechanical design
and layout of extrusion presses.

Morris Electronics
Manufacturer crossbar switches, scanners, monitors. Assigned to
design and layout of electronic devices.

Milo Corp./Simco Electric Co./Western Conductor Sales
Manufacturers portable and mobile testing equipment for missile and
aircraft industries; manufacturers electronic components for missile,
aircraft, radio, and television industries.

In above employments, duties involved: layout, design of electro-
mechanical parts and devices for ground support of drone target
planes, plus modernization of obsolete drawings, pictorial views of
components for mechanical and electrical parts lists.

Burns Electronics
Manufacturer missiles and component parts. Revised old drawings,
detailed new layouts. Did schematics, wiring diagrams, pictorial
drawings, electrical parts lists, wire lists; detailed instrument
panels.

REFERENCES ON REQUEST

Synopsis of Resume of:
DONALD FREER

27 Meigs St.
Olympia, WA 98501
Phone: (507) 366-3228

JOB OBJECTIVE

Field of electronics on technician level with growth opportunity

EMPLOYMENT

1982-Present	MANVILLE-FORBES CO., Portland, OR Service engineer for North America Note: Continuation of employment next below: company sold out to Manville-Forbes Co.
1980-1982	ACE AUTOMATION CO., Culver City, CA Service Manager
1974-1979	BORGMAN CORPORATION, Sacramento, CA Supervisor of mechanical maintenance
Prior	KELLER FORD AGENCY, Carson City, NV Auto mechanic plus all radio repair
	U.S. FORESTRY SERVICE Mechanic supervising repair of road-building equipment. Left to seek position in industry.
General:	Can operate or repair any type of machine in a standard machine shop.

EDUCATION

Formal:	Franklin Technical Institute, Geyser, NV Machine Design. Graduated. Culver Institute of Technology: (Evening Course) Sacramento, CA: Industrial Management.
Other:	LaSalle Technical Institute (Correspondence) NYC, NY: Radio and Electronics. Extensive home study in electricity and electronics.

PERSONAL

Born:	5/4/45. Married. Two children. Health: excellent.
Residence:	Rents home; free to relocate.
Hobbies:	Hunting; fishing; model railroading.

(FOR AMPLIFICATION SEE FOLLOWING)

Demonstrating experience equivalent to education accepted by many employers in lieu of college. Steady position climb clearly indicates conscientious application of knowledge acquired on the job.

Amplified Resume   Donald Freer
                                                      -page 2-

EMPLOYMENT HIGHLIGHTS

1980-Present
MANVILLE-FORBES CO. and
ACE AUTOMATION CO.

Employed originally by Ace Automation Co. to service and install
electrically operated continuous weighing systems produced by the
company.

In 1982 company sold out to Manville-Forbes Co. Company retained
and ultimately promoted him to Service Engineer for all of North
America. Installations run into high six figures. He supervises
each one; trains servicepeople in the local Manville-Forbes offices
in all aspects of repair and service.

  Results:
  Has accomplished his installations and training programs to the
  complete satisfaction of customers and company. Has outstanding
  record of no complaints - no record of faulty installations or
  poor service.

Reason for desiring change: Vast territory requires absence from
home for several months at a time. Would change to a position permitting more time with family.

1974-1979
BORGMAN CORPORATION

Employed as one of 10 maintenance machinists repairing all types of
machine shop equipment.

Promoted to Supervisor of Maintenance of Mechanical Equipment with
up to 15 personnel under his direction. Was charged with responsibility of keeping machinery and vehicles running in a plant employing from 1500 in slow periods, to 2000 at peak, on each shift.
Machinery ranged from simple machine shop devices to highly complicated special machines. For example, electrical or mechanical
equipment used in modern medical laboratories.

Interviewed and recommended employment of his assistants; discharged
when necessary. Trained his people when skilled personnel were not
available. Relations with personnel excellent, with low turnover.
Separations normally occurred as a result of company's fluctuating
volume.

Has excellent letters of reference attesting to leadership ability
specifically emphasizing consistently good record of turning un-
trained and/or poor workmen into good producers. Left for better
position after company reorganization.

References available

Synopsis of Resume of:
HAROLD KNOWLAND

876 Highland Drive
Seattle, WA 98013
Phone: (206) 972-8762

JOB OBJECTIVE

Design Engineering in Electromechanical Field

EMPLOYMENT

1981-Present   GENERAL PACIFIC, INC., Seattle, WA
                Income has increased by $8,000 since joining company.
                Machine designer

1980-1981   DELCO ENGINEERING CO., Boise, ID
                Contract design work

1978-1980   ALLSTATE TOOL MACHINE CO., Silver City, ID
                Detailer. Actual work was in electromech. design.

Prior   FOTEX, INC., Silver City, ID
                Draftsman

EDUCATION

1973-1976   University of Southern California
                   Degree: three years' study toward BS in Mechanical
                Engineering. Compelled to leave for reasons of
                health.

1978-1980   Silver Springs Institute of Technology, Silver City, ID
                   Associate degree in design engineering, acquired
                   through night school attendance.

Other: Company-sponsored course on automation.

PERSONAL

Born: 10/10/54. Married; two children; good health.
Hobbies: Do-it-yourself home projects; music.
Affiliations: Allstate Society of Design Engineers.

(FOR AMPLIFICATION SEE FOLLOWING)

*Good employment record complicated by poor health factor, which cannot be
ignored, but need not be dwelled upon. "Warmer climate" reason for leaving present
employment is on advice of physician. Inasmuch as warmer climate will solve
physical problems, it is better to limit resume geographical scope than to point up
health aspect.*

Amplified Resume

Harold Knowland
-page 2-

EMPLOYMENT HIGHLIGHTS

1981-Present
GENERAL PACIFIC, INC., Seattle, WA
(Mechanical packings and oil seals)

Employed as machine designer in a company which requires special machines for unusual products.

Given an idea or request for a machine to perform a specific function, works out an original idea. Makes rough sketch and rough estimate. If approved, makes complete layout sketch of the device; has a detail worker prepare the final drawings. Then follows through construction of device in the shop until it is put to actual production use. Has final decision on any suggested changes.

Results:
Has worked on the design of 70 machines; has completed approximately 30 since joining the company. Has had several notable successes. (1) Design of impregnated packing, folding and calendering machines. (2) Machine to deliver rubber in varying plies. (3) Trimming machines for shaft seal inserts, more versatile, fast, and accurate than formerly possible.

Reason for desiring change: Warmer climate.

1980-1981
DELCO ENGINEERING CO., Boise, ID

Employed with expectation of design work. Did not develop. Resigned to accept better position above.

1978-1980
ALLSTATE TOOL MACHINE CO., Silver City, ID

Employed in capacity as "Detailer," contacted customers, did electro-mechanical design, including relay work. Company financial reverses resulted in drastic cut in work force, and position was eliminated.

PRIOR

Following college was employed in radio repair shop while recuperating from an illness ultimately diagnosed as an allergy; fully arrested. Accepted various jobs as draftsman prior to above employment.

General

In recent aptitude and ability tests given by present company, scored 8th of 125 persons working in same area.

References available

Synopsis of Resume of:
HELMUT L. DAMSKY

22 Tyler Rd.
So. Providence, RI 02910
Phone: (401) 882-7664

JOB OBJECTIVE

Position in Mechanical Engineering or Design

EMPLOYMENT

1980-Present
VICE PRESIDENT and GENERAL MANAGER
Neely Equipment Co. (Division of National Packaging
Corp.)
Providence, RI

1980-Present
PLANT ENGINEER (simultaneous with above)
National Packaging Corp., Providence, RI

1975-1980
TOOL and DIE FOREMAN
Haverhill Instruments Corp., Trenton, NJ

1972-1975
TOOL ROOM SUPERVISOR
Elgin Machine Corp., New Haven, CT

EDUCATION

1971-1972
Providence Technical Institute, Providence, RI
Course in Organic Chemistry and Basic Radio.

Other:
Rhode Island College, Providence, RI (Evening Courses)
Management, Economics, Mathematics.
Continuous self-study program in mechanics, engineer-
ing, electronics.
Has working knowledge of Polish and German languages.

PERSONAL

Born:
8/24/50 in Poland. Naturalized citizen of U.S. Married.
Health:
Excellent.
Hobbies:
Building stero components; photography; family
activities.
Affiliations:
Volunteer fire fighter.

(FOR AMPLIFICATION SEE FOLLOWING)

*Details given on major and longest employment only, to give emphasis to portion of
record where important progress has been made. It is assumed prospective
employer would be familiar with work involved in lesser employments; amplifications
could tend to detract from impact of more recent responsibilities and
accomplishments.*

Amplified Resume   Helmut L. Damsky
                                                      -page 2-

EMPLOYMENT HIGHLIGHTS

1980-Present
Neely Equipment Co.
(Manufacturers equipment for use in printing, coating, photo-engraving,
laminating, polyethelene extrusion)

   Employed originally by first parent company (Hunter Co. of Providence, RI), as an engineer in mechanical field. In 1981, Neely
   Equipment Co. was set up by the parent company; was made General
   Manager. 1982 elected Vice President. Both companies became division of National Packaging Corporation in 1984.

   Has all contact with prospective and established customers; discusses
   problems; implements solutions. Makes rough sketches of machines or
   devices; lays out proposed production line sequence. Upon approval,
   makes detailed drawings and estimates. After order is obtained,
   supervises production of equipment, sets up in customer's plant,
   follows through to employee training and full customer satisfaction.

   Equipment designed varies from normal mid-five-figure-cost to low
   six figures. Photographs and sketches of successful designs created
   are available for inspection.

   Results: Division has been profitable from start.

   Reason for leaving: Greater income.

1980-Present
National Packaging Corporation

   Added duties and responsibilities of Plant Engineer for National
   Packaging Corporation. Supervises polyethelene extrusion processes
   plus all mechanical and electrical maintenance.

   Hires and trains groups totaling 75 personnel for these purposes.
   Designs and redesigns equipment for better, more efficient, quality
   production. Supervises rebuilding, adds controls (both electrical
   and mechanical) for secondhand machinery brought into plant. Has
   achieved quality production with these machines formerly not ser-
   viceable.

REFERENCES

Available on request

Synopsis of Resume of:
THOMAS L. LYNN

98 Brooks Ave.
Boston, MA 02646
Phone: (617) 355-9877

JOB OBJECTIVE

Television Engineering Technician

EMPLOYMENT

1983-Present   WFPU-TV (PBS), Boston, MA
                  Engineering Technician

1981-1983   Kaymart Productions, Hollywood, CA
                  Design engineer assistant

1979-1981   Dell Fill Productions, Beverly Hills, CA
                  Photographer, Gaffer, Set Builder

EDUCATION

1975-1979   Boston University, Boston, MA
                  Majored in communications with emphasis
                  on broadcasting, production, and newswriting.

Other: Columbia College, Hollywood, CA
                  Courses in film production, sound
                  recording, and mixing.

PERSONAL

Born: 1945. Married.
Hobbies: Skiing; bridge; chess.
Affiliations: Jaycees; Knights of Columbus.

(FOR AMPLIFICATION SEE FOLLOWING)

Amplified Resume   Thomas L. Lynn
                                                         -page 2-

1983-Present
WFPU-TV, Boston, MA

    As engineering assistant, has been involved with production of the
    following:

        (1) Documentary films.
        (2) Weekly educational children's program.
        (3) Live television coverage of centennial.

    Familiar with:

        (1) RCA TK-43 and RCA-44B cameras.
        (2) RCA TR-70 video tape machine.
        (3) RCA TCR-100 cartridge video tape machine.
        (4) RCA TEP editor.
        (5) Character generator.
        (6) Camera and film chain; audio and video switching.
        (7) Studio lighting; operation of remote equipment.
        (8) Film editing.
        (9) Copywriting, trailer narration, mixing, gaffing.

    Reason for leaving: Limited opportunity. Currently studying for
    first class radio telephone license.

    Summary

    All previous experience has contributed to overall knowledge in
    chosen field. Has personally designed and built custom film editing
    equipment and projection devices, as well as custom dubbing studio.

                            REFERENCES

On request. Please do not contact present employer at this time.

Synopsis of Resume of: Care of C. Whitney
RUTH MALLORY   29 Gillette St.
                                                Richmond, VA 23234
                                                Phone: (703) 322-6647

JOB OBJECTIVE

Position as Executive Housekeeper: hotel, motel, apartment hotel

EXPERIENCE

1982-Present	500-room hotel located in eastern Virginia Salary $200.00 per week plus full maintenance Executive Housekeeper
1980-1982	HOTEL WAGNER, Norfolk, VA (300 rooms) Salary $150.00 per week, plus full maintenance Executive Housekeeper
1978-1980	CHATHAM HOTEL, Virginia Beach, VA (200 rooms) Salary $450 per month (no maintenance) Executive Housekeeper
1977	SEA CHEST HOTEL, Ft. Myers, FL (150 rooms) Salary $300 per month (plus apartment) Executive Housekeeper
1975-1977	NORMANDY APARTMENT HOTEL (75 rooms), New Orleans, LA Salary $300 per month (no maintenance) Executive Housekeeper

EDUCATION

Scholastic: Vocational school.

Special Training: Murey Hotel Training Course, Washington, D.C.
                       Courses in typing and bookkeeping - Niagara Falls,
                       Canada.

PERSONAL

Age: Mature. Health excellent.
Hobbies: Gardening; reading.
Affiliations: Executive Housekeepers Association.

(FOR AMPLIFICATION SEE FOLLOWING)

*As position title remains the same, progress is shown through increase in salary and
size of establishment. Because resume was to be widely circulated, actual name of
present hotel employment has been omitted. Mail address is that of relative rather
than hotel to prevent further identification.*

Amplified Resume   Ruth Mallory
                                                         -page 2-

EXPERIENCE

1982-Present
  As Executive Housekeeper for one of the leading hotels in eastern
  Virginia, has staff of 62 personnel under her supervision. Interviews, hires, trains, and has full right of discharge. Assigns all
  work, oversees its completion. Keeps time cards, records, and
  issues paychecks.

  Satisfactory discharge of multiple job duties has been complicated
  by complete redecoration and remodeling of the 500-room hotel, begun
  and continued during period of employment. Has had added responsibility of consultation and supervision of seamstress personnel, as
  well as deadlines to be met on rooms rented but not yet completed.
  Staff turnover has been held to a minimum, indicating excellent ability to maintain harmony and high morale despite trying conditions.

  Reason for desiring change: Salary not commensurate with responsibilities.

1980-82 HOTEL WAGNER (staff - 40)
  Executive Housekeeping functions similar to above on smaller scale,
  with added duties peculiar to a convention hotel. For example,
  tearing down bedrooms and remaking them into living rooms to accommo-
  date convention guests was weekly routine, often as many as 18-20
  per day. Resigned because of excessive strain.

1978-1980 CHATHAM HOTEL (staff - 35)
  Satisfactorily discharged assigned duties despite general employee
  strike called during her tenure. Temporary position which terminated when former housekeeper returned after leave of absence.

1977 SEA CHEST HOTEL (staff - 20)
  Employed as Executive Housekeeper with standard duties, plus full
  charge of laundry. Employment terminated when change in management
  brought in complete new staff.

1975-1977 NORMANDY APARTMENT HOTEL (staff - 20)
  Executive Housekeeping functions on small scale, plus doubling as
  evening receptionist. Left to return to Florida.

Prior
  Dealt with public in various capacities, including job of head hostess in the main dining room of the Sheraton-Brock Hotel in Niagara
  Falls, Canada. Successfully operated two restaurants in Florida,
  one with partner, one as sole owner. Sold both at profit.

REFERENCES

Available

Synopsis of Resume:
GARY M. SEIBERT

595 Ocean Blvd.
Sarasota, FL 33581
Phone: (813) 922-9875

JOB OBJECTIVE

Driving Instructor

EXPERIENCE

1981-Present: LUTHER'S DRIVING SCHOOL, Sarasota, FL
        Driving Instructor

1978-1981   MILLER FORD, Bradenton, FL
        Used car salesman

1970-1978   SARASOTA PUBLIC SCHOOLS
        Elementary school teacher

EDUCATION

1966-1969   University of Alabama, Tuscaloosa, AL
        B.A. Sociology; minor - Political Science.

Other: Self-initiated tour of California, and southwestern
        U.S. for independent study of car rallying immediately
        following graduation.

PERSONAL

Born: 1947   Single parent; two teenagers; health excellent.
Hobbies: Tennis; golf; sports car rallying; hang gliding; flying.

Skills: Chauffeur's License, private pilot's license.

(FOR AMPLIFICATION SEE FOLLOWING)

Single parent changing fields of employment later in career.

Amplified Resume

Gary M. Seibert
-page 2-

EXPERIENCE

1981-Present
LUTHER'S DRIVING SCHOOL

Employed as instructor for this commercial driving school, which has enjoyed an excellent reputation for past 20 years in the area. Employees subject to intensive screening, as well as required to pass stringent state requirements as follows.

State of Florida requires completion of a 32-hour course in driver education approved by Division of Driver Licenses. Encompasses intensive written test based on Florida Driver's Handbook, and rules and regulations governing commercial driving schools.

During any consecutive three-year period, every driver instructor must maintain a driving record which does not include more than three chargeable accidents or violations. Any violation will result in suspension or revocation and will automatically cause cancellation of the instructor's certificate.

All instructors required to attend a refresher course in driver education approved by state every five years. Applicant may not have been convicted of a felony or any crime involving violence, or have engaged in any dishonest, indecent, or immoral conduct.

Tests approximately four students daily, and occasionally on weekends. Age of students range from teenagers to senior citizens upward to age 85. Lessons are of two-hour duration on the average; success rate of students passing their state driving examination road and written tests on first try has been approximately 90%.

Reason for desiring change: Personal reasons to be discussed at interview.

FORMER EMPLOYMENTS
Teacher
Taught social studies in public schools, resigning voluntarily following divorce. Excellent references and record during tenure.

Car salesman
Successfully sold used cars and trucks for agency, named "Top Salesman" last year of employment. Amicable separation to accept position which would combine teaching and driving skills.

REFERENCES

Available on request; present employer may be contacted.

Synopsis of Resume of: 440 Ridgewood Ave.
JANICE R. EASTWOOD   Annandale, VA 24422
                                                 Phone: (703) 987-4557

JOB OBJECTIVE

Retirement Complex Management

EMPLOYMENT

1982-Present   ENDICOTT RETIREMENT COMPLEX, Annandale, VA
                Low-income housing, 94 units. Resident Manager

Prior   Part-time summer employments while in college: Busch
                Gardens, Williamsburg, VA: guest relations hostess,
                hospitality hostess, cashier.

EDUCATION

1978-1982   Radford University, Radford, VA
                   Degree: B.A. - Social work; Minor - Psychology.
                Honors:
                   Alpha Delta Mu (National Social Work Honor Society);
                   Pi Gamma Nu (National Social Sciences Honor Society);
                   Vice President of National Federation of Student
                   Social Workers.

Other: Institute of Real Estate Management, 101 Series.
                   Educational Requirement for accredited Resident
                   Manager Designation.
                Burrell Home for Adults, Roanoke, VA.
                   Total 400 hrs. exposure in adult home setting.
                   Included: ambulatory, non-ambulatory, mentally and
                   physically handicapped. Developed recreational
                   activity; expanded volunteer program; counseled
                   residents.
                Radford University.
                   Upon graduation served as social work intern for
                   six weeks.

PERSONAL

Age: 26; single; excellent health; willing to relocate.
Hobbies: Outdoor sports; needlework; art.
Affiliations: League of Older Americans: retired Senior Volunteer
               Program; Advisory Council Member; United Way Council
               member.

(FOR AMPLIFICATION SEE FOLLOWING)

Amplified Resume   Janice R. Eastwood
                                                          -page 2-

EMPLOYMENT HIGHLIGHTS

<u>1982-Present</u>
<u>ENDICOTT RETIREMENT COMPLEX</u>

Selected from multiple applicants shortly after graduation from college
as resident manager of this 94-unit apartment complex by Management
Services of Silver Springs, VA, whose function is to manage and staff
this and similar complexes for owners.

Responsible for employment and supervision of qualified personnel, as
well as training and performance review of three staff persons: secretary, janitor, and maintenance.

Daily, ongoing responsibilities include:

(1) Rental of apartments to low-income persons over 62 years of age,
and younger disabled persons who meet eligibility criteria of HUD.

(2) Prospective tenant interviews; determination of eligibility; credit
and reference checks. Rental collections; bank deposits; purchases of
supplies; janitorial needs, repair costs, office supplies.

(3) Supervision, general administration and physical operation of complex. After completion and initial occupancy of building, responsible
for warranty issues and consultation with general contractor on construction and maintenance issues.

(4) On 24-hour call, charged with successfully meeting and handling all
medical and maintenance emergencies. Full charge of all complex social
activities and resident relations as well as supervision of staff providing transportation, recreational, and housekeeping services to resi-
dents.

(5) Charged with marketing and ultimate lease signing of all apartments.
Advertises and promotes elderly housing life-style options through bulk
mailings and personal presentations to community groups and organizations.

<u>R e s u l t s</u>:
Has experienced no turnover in immediate staff; tenant morale high;
each six-month evaluation from supervisor rated "Excellent" with appropriate raise in salary.

<u>Reason for desiring change</u>: Would make change to larger market with
potential for upward career move.

REFERENCES

Available on request. Please do not contact present employer
                         at this time.

Synopsis of Resume of: 530 Marion Ave.
PETER AVERY   Dallas, TX 78745
                                             (512) 972-0733

JOB OBJECTIVE

Condominium or apartment complex management in state of Texas

EXPERIENCE

1977-Present	OAK PLAZA VILLAS, Dallas, TX 58 one-story units, in three sections. Manager
1971-1977	HAUSER REALTY, INC., Fort Worth, TX Real Estate Sales and property management
1969-1971	MORGAN DEPARTMENT STORE, Gaylord, LA Clerk to Assistant Buyer
1965-1968	Miscellaneous employment as carpenter and construction worker.

EDUCATION

1963-1965	Vocational-Technical Institute, Beaumont, TX Shop and automotive mechanics.
Other:	High school; correspondence accounting course; refresher bookkeeping course nights at community college.
Skills:	Carpentry, drywall work, plumbing, bricklaying, mechanics.

PERSONAL

Born:	1940; single; good health; willing to relocate within state.
Hobbies:	Making furniture; softball; bowling.
Affiliations:	Lions Club; Red Cross volunteer.

(FOR AMPLIFICATION SEE FOLLOWING)

Amplified Resume   Peter Avery
                                                          -page 2-

EMPLOYMENT HIGHLIGHTS

1977-Present
OAK PLAZA VILLAS

Offered position as manager of this 58-unit complex, inheriting chaotic
situation due to incompetence of two former managers.

Completely reorganized books; installed new system of billing, bookkeeping, record keeping, and bill paying. Repaired outdoor furniture
in recreation area, erected pool fence, and changed filter system.

Streamlined rental procedures of owner-investor units, requiring prospective tenant-rental application forms complete with current references. Assumed responsibility for checking references as well as
interviewing prospects and presenting Board of Directors with findings
for final decisions.

With volunteer resident labor and cooperation, effected complete reno-
vation of recreation room, large common area used for meetings and
social activities. Repainted, recarpeted, installed new lighting
system both in and out for improved security; installed bolt locks.

Get bids for periodic projects such as roofing, septic tank cleaning,
and paving for final board decision. Oversees trash collection, pest
control operators, and serves as general troubleshooter in tenant dis-
putes.

Does all banking; makes daily check of laundromat appliances in each
of three buildings, as well as evening check for any trouble alert.
Fields phone calls for proper referrals; organizes monthly and annual
board meetings.

Overall running responsibilities encompass: billing, annual report,
bookkeeping, collection of delinquent accounts, and assessments.

Reason for desiring change: Remuneration inconsistent with duties
and responsibilities; prefer rent-free apartment or condominium in
addition to salary.

REFERENCES

On request

Synopsis of Resume of: 756 Tangelo Ave.
JOHN D. FOLEY   Orange City, FL 32763
                                                 Phone: (813) 397-7765

OBJECTIVE

Security Guard

EXPERIENCE

6/84-Present   LAKE WOODS RETIREMENT CENTER, Orange City, FL
                      Security Guard

1978-1984   WAKEFIELD CORPORATION, FL
                      Polygraph Examiner

1951-1979   DEPARTMENT OF POLICE, Union, NJ
                      From foot patrol to Bureau of Criminal
                      Investigation to Detective and Supervisor

1946-1951   CUMMINGS PHOTOGRAPHY, New York City
                      Commercial Photography

EDUCATION

1937-Present

High school graduate; continuous field-related seminars in: polygraph
science; law enforcement; video application for security; narcotics;
Firearms Instructors School.

Other:
Recently passed Sharpshooter Test as present job requirement; owns
38 magnum pistol. Registered N.R.A. Police Pistol Instructor.

PERSONAL

Age: 57, married, two grown children, good health; 20/20 vision with
glasses.

Service: Marine Corps: - Guadalcanal, Solomon Islands 1941-45.

(FOR AMPLIFICATION SEE FOLLOWING)

*Older career police officer using past good record as qualification for security job in
retirement.*

Amplified Resume

John D. Foley
-page 2-

EXPERIENCE HIGHLIGHTS

6/84 Present
LAKE WOODS RETIREMENT CENTER

Accepted low-stress job as security job while recuperating from operation. From guardhouse at gate, checks all persons entering for proper authorization, including all automobiles and commercial vehicles. Records all information; reports any irregularities or disturbances to "round sergeant" who makes physical checks of residences.

Is required to remain at post for round-the-clock security, working shifts of 4-12, 12-8, 8-4, as scheduled. Uniforms furnished.

Reason for desiring change: More responsibility consistent with background.

1978-1984
WAKEFIELD CORPORATION

Employed as state licensed examiner for detection of deception in polygraphs. Conducted pre-employment, periodic and specific polygraph examinations for large numbers and wide range of occupations of company's large client roster. Analyzed charts; made critical decisions as to truthfulness or deception. Left for bypass operation.

1951-1979
DEPARTMENT OF POLICE, UNION, NJ

1951 - Foot patrol, radio car patrol, motorcycle, and dispatch officer.

1954 - Promoted to Bureau of Criminal Investigation. Established classification system; police photographer for criminal and accident investigation; court fingerprint expert witness; two citations for valor in apprehension of two murder suspects.

1975 - Promoted to General Supervisor of all Record Personnel. Duties encompassed: preservation and documentation of physical evidence and property; preparation of forensic material; investigation and preparation of firearm purchase and concealed weapon permits.

Reason for leaving: Retired to Florida for better climate.

REFERENCES

Available, as well as commendations.

Synopsis of Resume of
ANTHONY J. MICELLI

5007 Bristol Ave.
Sioux Falls, SD 57105
Phone: (605) 729-1062

JOB OBJECTIVE

Superintendent of Construction, or Carpenter's Superintendent

EMPLOYMENT

6/85-Present   CARPENTER (fill-in position)
                J. Ackerman & Son, Sioux Falls, SD

6/83-12/84   GENERAL SUPERINTENDENT ($4-million apartment house)
                Regal Homes, Inc., Sioux Falls, SD

3/82-5/83   GENERAL CONSTRUCTION SUPERINTENDENT
                Hastings Contracting Co., Aberdeen, SD

1/81-2/82   CONSTRUCTION SUPERINTENDENT ($1,000,000 apartment house)
                Lindsay Construction Co., Bismark, ND

1971-1980   GENERAL SUPERINTENDENT, CARPENTER SUPERINTENDENT,
                CARPENTER FOREMAN
                Blanchard Construction Co., Bismark, ND

1970-1980   SELF-EMPLOYED - home builder
                Pierre, SD, area

Prior   Began work as part-time laborer during high school
                period; served apprenticeship as carpenter with Elmer
                D. Smith & Sons, Cheyenne, WY

EDUCATION

High School: Cheyenne Sr. High School, Cheyenne, WY. Graduated 1969.
Other: Served apprenticeship (above); completed all required
                   work.
                Bismarck Technical School (attended nights)
                   Blueprint Reading and Estimating.

PERSONAL

Born: 10/4/51; married, four school-age children.
Health: Excellent.
Hobbies: Hunting; fishing; gardening.
Affiliations: Carpenters Union, church member.

(FOR AMPLIFICATION SEE FOLLOWING)

*Field where short-term employment listing need not be avoided, for "project
completed" is accepted as standard and sufficient reason for employment
termination. Basic skills shown through early on-the-job training, as well as through
variety of jobs satisfactorily completed. Range of supervisory capability demonstrated
by cost of projects successfully completed.*

Amplified Resume

Anthony J. Micelli
-page 2-

EMPLOYMENT HIGHLIGHTS

6/85-Present
J. ACKERMAN & SONS

Accepted carpenter's position while seeking more responsible post in line with skills and experience outlined below.

6/83-12/84
REGAL HOMES, INC.

Employed as General Superintendent of the construction of the "Skyline" apartment house (a $4,000,000, four-floor, 90-apartment, brick and block building with brick veneer).

Had complete supervision of the entire operation. Directed a total of 90 workers in all trades. Directly supervised carpenters and masons, including installation of storm and sanitary sewers. Oversaw the subcontracted work in plumbing, electrical, steel, and heating. Purchased mason materials and carpenter requirements.

Results: Project completed four months ahead of schedule.
         No labor group difficulties; no repercussions.

Reason for leaving: Work completed; no other project in progress.

3/82-5/83
HASTINGS CONTRACTING CO.

Employed as general construction superintendent. Handled such projects as: building remodeling, manhole construction, roads, water lines, etc. Had as many as four jobs under way simultaneously with varying number of workers according to project requirements.

Reason for leaving: Work completed; no new projects on hand.

1/81-2/82
LINDSAY CONSTRUCTION CO.

Employed as Construction Superintendent directing mason and carpentry work of up to 85 workers. Hired, laid off (through a foreman), the following: carpenters, masons, laborers.

Results: Built a $1,000,000 apartment house ahead of schedule and at a profit.

Reason for leaving: Profits not sufficient to support six company heads; company liquidated.

References on request

Synopsis of Resume of:
SHERMAN T. CONKLIN

542 Langley Rd.
Great Falls, MT 59401
Phone: (406) 781-8664

JOB OBJECTIVE

General Contractor

EXPERIENCE

1981-Present	Self-employed - General Contractor Conklin & Son Construction Company, Great Falls, MT
1978-1981	Self-employed - General Contractor Partnership, Casper, WY
1970-1978	Miscellaneous employments in Cheyenne, WY: milling machine operator, operator heavy highway equipment, construction work (mason, carpenter). Left to attend Haxton Institute (see Education).

EDUCATION

1968-1970   Haxton Institute, Olympia, WA
    Full-time, two-year course in Building Construction.
    Graduated 3rd in class of 47.
Other: International Correspondence School
    Architectural Course.
    Casper High School, Casper, WY
    Adult Education courses in Real Estate Appraisal,
    Business Law, Accounting (nights).
    Eastern Montana College of Education, Billings, MT
    Advanced Course for Home Builders.
    (Summer Session).
    Builders Management Seminars:
    Olympia, WA; San Francisco, CA; Chicago, IL;
    New York, NY.
Current: Continuous self-study (technical periodicals, etc.)

PERSONAL

Born: 4/19/50. Health: excellent.
Residence: Owns home; will relocate within state.
Affiliations: Great Falls Home Builders Association.

(FOR AMPLIFICATION PLEASE SEE FOLLOWING)

Multiple educational courses listed in detail on synopsis sheet to gain full, favorable impact of continual efforts to add to, and acquire, current know-how. Amplification has slight sales-public relations slant so that resume can be used in field other than listed under job objectives.

EXPERIENCE

SELF-EMPLOYED

1978-1981
Following completion of Haxton Institute formed partnership in Casper, WY, employing about 10 personnel to take painting contracts. Continued painting activities, expanding to include mason and carpenter contracting. Profitable operation; sold out to partner to go into business with own son.

1981
Formed own business in Great Falls, MT, a faster growing area, subcontracting for various developers. Had up to 50 employees on weekly payroll. Also construction superintendent for community center project.

1982
Expanded business to include small commercial, sewer, water line work, building, electrical, carpentry, and masonry.

1983
Became General Contractor. Builds standard homes and small commercial buildings. Contracts range from $40,000 to $500,000. Does own sewer and water line work, masonry, plumbing, carpentry, and painting.

Personally does all selling (is licensed real estate salesperson). Contracts architects, brokers, finance officers of lending institutions, and prospective clients. Does all estimating (has consistently been within 1% to 2%). Is familiar with mortgage procedures, bank lending, real estate codes, building codes, and has had up to 10 projects under way simultaneously in different locations.

To assist in proper building, developed a plan or estimate sheet which has been discussed and favorably commented upon by other builders. Maintains a flow sheet of work progress indicating materials and money required at estimated times.

Gets along well with workers, many of whom have been employed by firm since business was formed. Is highly regarded by local officials, and is comfortable dealing with authority at all levels.

Reason for desiring change:
Have progressed as far as possible under existing setup. Have no time to assume the additional responsibilities necessary for expansion.

REFERENCES

Available

Synopsis of Resume of: 74 Atkins St.
STANLEY R. MORAN   Nashville. TN 37205
                                                Phone: (615) 431-7651

JOB OBJECTIVE

Position in supervision on foreman level, in charge of punch
press, grinding or machine shop

EMPLOYMENT

1979-Present   ACE SIGNAL CORP. (over 1,000 employees)
except for   12 Market St., Nashville, TN
period next   Foreman of Punch Press, Grinding, Gear Cutting Depts.
below   (Presently has temporary position as tool and die
                   maker; see amplification for details).

1980-1982   GLEASON MANUFACTURING CO. (500 employees)
                300 West 50th St., Knoxville, TN
                   Tool and Die Maker

Prior   Assistant manager family owned restaurant in Atlanta,
                GA. Profitable operation; left when restaurant was sold.

EDUCATION

High School: Fulton Senior High School, Atlanta GA

Other: Brewer Business Academy, Atlanta, GA
(Nights)   Bookkeeping and Accounting Course.
                Winslow Technical Institute
                   Machine shop courses for apprenticeship.
                Tenn. Agricultural & Industrial State University
                   Courses included: Drafting, Blueprint Reading,
                   Mathematics, Business Management, Personnel Management

PERSONAL

Born: 2/24/51. Married; two children; health--good.
Residence: Owns home; would relocate for right opportunity.
Hobbies: Hunting; fishing; softball.

(FOR AMPLIFICATION SEE FOLLOWING)

*Amplified as a one-employment record to point up solid background in field of
present job objective. Brief listing of former employments adequately fulfills purpose
of showing steadiness of work history.*

Amplified Resume   Stanley R. Moran
                                                        -page 2-

EMPLOYMENT

1979-Present (except for 80-82)
ACE SIGNAL CORP. - manufacturers signals, air
traffic and vehicular systems and devices.

1979   Originally employed as tool crib attendant. Began and completed
        as machinist. Remained as machinist until 1975; left to accept
        greater income position offered by Gleason Manufacturing Co.
        Worked as tool and die maker, engaged in making parts for pre-
        cision instruments until company terminated operations 6/82.

7/82   Returned to Ace Signal Corp. as a tool and die maker. Remained
        in that capacity until 1983, when company paid for complete
        tests of aptitudes at Tenn. State University Testing Center.

        Selected for promotion to Foreman of the Punch Press Dept., con-
        sisting of: fourteen operators, five sheet metal workers and
        three set-up men. At three different periods a second shift was
        added, giving authority over approximately forty personnel at
        maximum.

        Utilized heavy, medium, and light presses, working with steel,
        brass, bronze, silver, and other metals. Work ranged from
        pressing heavy metal for railroad equipment to small high-pre-
        cision work for electrical devices.

        In overall departmental reorganization, the Grinding and Gear
        Cutting Departments were added to job responsibilities. Grind-
        ing Department operated cylindrical, rotary, and surface grind-
        ers; Gear Cutting Dept. was concerned with gear cutting and
        broaching.

        Did all interviewing, hiring, and training of replacement person-
        nel. Record of accomplishment during entire supervisory period
        shows:

        (1) Work regularly completed on schedule.
        (2) Low rejection record.
        (3) Minimum of personnel problems brought to Grievance Committee.
        (4) Minimum customer complaints.

1984   Further consolidation of departments resulted in the group being
        absorbed in the larger milling and drilling group, with a Senior
        Foreman taking over.

Reason for desiring change: Has remained with company on an interim
basis as tool and die maker while seeking position which would fully
utilize training, ability, and experience.

REFERENCES AVAILABLE

Synopsis of Resume of: 12 Kaiser Ave.
PHILIP C. CONWELL   Boise, ID 83702
                                                Phone: (208) 820-3001

JOB OBJECTIVE

Plant Manager or Supervision leading to Management position

EMPLOYMENT

1979-Present   GENERAL MANAGER
                Greer Manufacturing Co., Boise, ID
                (Manufacturers food handling equipment)

1976-1979   PRODUCTION CONTROL EXPEDITER
                Hadden Meter Company, Boise, ID (1,000 employees)
                Resigned to accept position offer from above company.

Prior   Summer employments during college period:
                machine shop assistant, construction worker, etc.

EDUCATION

1972-1976   Montana State University, Missoula, MT
                    Degree: B.S. in Business Administration.

SERVICE

1968-1972   U.S. Navy. Aviation Cadet to Ensign. Served as Flight
                Instructor and Aide to Commanding Officer.
                Honorably Released. Not in Reserves.

PERSONAL

Born: 7/25/48. Health--good.
Hobbies: Hunting; fishing; golf.
Affiliations: Chamber of Commerce; church member; political club
                (past president).

(FOR AMPLIFICATION SEE FOLLOWING)

*Responsibilities of major employment classified to demonstrate ability to cope with
wide range of problems involved in small plant management. Major plant expediting
(indicated by number of employees) important to well-rounded plant experience.
However, as details of such work would be familiar to prospective employers in this
field, they are omitted.*

Amplified Resume   Philip C. Conwell
                                                    -page 2-

EMPLOYMENT HIGHLIGHTS

1979-Present
GREER MANUFACTURING COMPANY

Employed originally as Assistant General Manager; in two years promoted to General Manager.

Business is family-owned and specializes in such products as complete handling centers for potatoes, onions, etc. Centers consist
of graders, washers, conveyors, etc. Some combinations reach 75
feet in length with single installations selling in substantial five-
figure sums. Other items are designed and produced to perform special operations. Plant fabrication includes steel and wood with
complete shop facilities for both mediums.

As General Manager, has complete charge of plant and production.
Hires, fires, and directs a continuing training program for new employees. Responsibilities extend beyond plant, and include:

(1) Sales
    Acting through dealers, does considerable work assisting them by
    actual customer contact. Makes direct sales.

(2) Prospectus
    Surveys problem to be solved; makes initial sketches, followed
    by actual design and layout. Develops cost of components and
    fabrication; purchases required materials or components.

(3) Supervision
    Supervises construction, and designates crew to follow shipment
    and assembly in purchasers' plant. In the event of operating
    problems after installation, makes personal check to find and
    implement solution.

(4) Public Relations
    Excellent relations with plant personnel; has won cooperation
    and maximum effort. Good customer relations, successfully over-
    coming problems resulting from lack of technical skills in cus-
    tomer personnel.

Results: Work has resulted in the plant's achieving a high profit
volume.

Reason for desiring change: Have reached highest possible level in
family-operated business; would change for broader opportunity.

REFERENCES AVAILABLE

Synopsis of Resume of:
IRWIN E. DAILEY

17 Orchard Place
Houston, TX 77006
Phone: (713) 514-7443

JOB OBJECTIVE

Position as Production Control Manager

EMPLOYMENT

1979-8/85
PRODUCTION CONTROL SUPERINTENDENT
Ames Lumber Products Corporation
Houston, TX

1975-1979
SENIOR STAFF CONSULTANT
Swenson Management Advisory Consultants, Inc.
98 East 14th St., Chicago Heights, IL

1970-1975
HEAD OF PLANNING (moved up through stages from machinist)
Clinton Machine Co., Columbus, OH

EDUCATION

1966-1970
Tiffin University, Tiffin, OH
    Degree: B.S. in Commerce
    Expenses: Earned approximately 50%.
    Honors: Dean's List last two semesters.

Other:
Clinton Machine Company: Management courses; computer courses. Yearly seminars in San Francisco, CA, sponsored by present company.

PERSONAL

Born: 8/10/46. Married, two children in college.
Health: Good.
Hobbies: Hunting; swimming; golf.
Affiliations: American Production & Control Society;
               Chamber of Commerce.

(FOR AMPLIFICATION SEE FOLLOWING)

Solid background picture achieved through specifics of present position, as well as through general detail of former ones. Reasons for leaving excellent position were of personal nature, better explained at interview.

Amplified Resume

Irwin E. Dailey
-page 2-

EMPLOYMENT HIGHLIGHTS

1979-8/85
AMES LUMBER PRODUCTS CORP.

Employed as Production Control Manager with the specific assignment of establishing a three-plant unified corporate production control organization.

Organization was completed, tying in sales forecasts on stock and special orders, outside warehousing on nationwide basis, with proper stocks for prompt customer service, scheduling of production and shipments, and appropriate raw material purchasing. Task complicated by rapid company growth (from three to six plants and individual plant company growth).

In 1977 a crash decentralization was begun, with an independent department in each of six plants. Was made Production Control Superintendent of headquarters plant in Houston, Texas. Established model department to be followed by other plants. Departments were separate except for stock warehouse inventory tie-in.

Now directs a department of 110 workers controlling the following: scheduling, order processing, shipping, traffic, receiving, warehousing, inventory control, and purchasing, for a plant of 900 workers with productive volume in substantial seven figures.

Results: 1.   Staff trained in corporate setup has taken over other plants; workers presently in training at Houston slated for department head positions.

            2.   All standards set by management have been met or exceeded; low turnover of department personnel.

            3.   20% salary increase, plus bonuses.

Reason for leaving: To be discussed at interview.

REFERENCES

Available

Synopsis of Resume of: 44 Holly Rd.
HAROLD J. BEALE   Salem, OR 97306
                                                    Phone: (503) 421-8753

JOB OBJECTIVE

Shop Supervision, Welding Foreman, Instructor in Welding

EMPLOYMENT

1980-Present   SPECIALTY WELDER, WELDER FOREMAN
                 Cooper-Noonan Div. Salem Steel, Inc.
                 Salem, OR

1975-1980   SELF-EMPLOYED - owner welding shop and welding school.

Prior   Farm work during high school period.

EDUCATION

Wolf Point High School, Wolf Point, MT
   Graduated.
Makey Welding School, Boise, ID. 1975
   One-year welding course, included acetylene welding.
Other:
   I.C.S. Welding Course, varied safety and miscellane-
   ous company courses.

PERSONAL

Born: 1/5/47. Married; good health.
Hobbies: Restoring antique cars; camping.
Civic: Active in various civic and church fund-raising drives,
             has been chairman of several.

(FOR AMPLIFICATION SEE FOLLOWING)

Level of supervisory responsibility shown through number of persons supervised;
success of effort shown through promotion.

Amplified Resume   Harold J. Beale
                                                         -page 2-

EMPLOYMENT

1980-Present
COOPER-NOONAN - Division of Salem Steel, Inc.

Originally employed in Template Shop as helper, moved to multiple
punch helper to welder.

Promoted to Welding Inspector; served as sole plant inspector to
320 welders.

Promoted to Foreman (approximately 50 welders) in Marine Division
of Salem Steel.

Appointed Navy Yard Instructor for new welders. Note: Was also
training welders in own shop and school at request of the company.
Total working hours: approximately 15 hours per day, 7 days per
week.

Appointed welding Foreman on Navy Yard Outfitting Docks. Employed
in this capacity until returning to plant as Specialty Welder when
navy work slowed down.

Continues to serve as Specialty and Acetylene welder, considered to
be plant's specialist or expert welder. Collaborates with engineering department in tests of new varieties of welding materials;
assists in making decisions on recommended changes.

Reason for desiring change: Feels future prospects in steel industry uncertain. Would make change anywhere (including overseas) for
connection with progressive company.

REFERENCES

Personal references available on request.
Please do not contact present company until after interview.

Synopsis of Resume of:
GERALD L. MAURER

76 Caldwell St.
Binghamton, NY 13903
Phone: (716) 643-3419

JOB OBJECTIVE

Position as Tool Engineer or related activity

EMPLOYMENT

1978-Present	TOOL ENGINEER Ansco, Binghamton, NY (1,500 employees. Producers of: color photographic film, microfilm, copy papers, etc.)
1971-1978	FOREMAN (tool and die group) - moved up from apprentice. Marx Tool & Gauge Co., Trenton, NJ (Largest shop of kind on East Coast.)

EDUCATION

East High School, Allentown, PA
  Graduate. President of class Jr. year.
Tool and Die Making Apprenticeship.
  Completed all courses including blueprint reading.
Misc.:   Moderate knowledge of German; excellent command of English.

PERSONAL

Born: 7/2/43. Married, two children. Health: excellent.
Hobbies: Baseball (capt. softball team); bowling; camping.
Affiliations: American Legion; church member.

(FOR AMPLIFICATION SEE FOLLOWING)

Despite lack of formal training, applicant demonstrates high degree of self-development, as shown by level of responsibility and concrete dollars-and-cents results. Reason for leaving could not be briefly stated; is best omitted, to be discussed at interview.

Amplified Resume

Gerald L. Maurer
-page 2-

EMPLOYMENT HIGHLIGHTS

1978-Present
ANSCO

Employed as Tool Engineer with responsibilities that include the following:

Direction of machine shop.

Determination of equipment required to handle foreseeable production.

Development of cost of necessary equipment, practicability of production within company or farming to outside vendors.

Assistance in preparation of drawings and data necessary for producing equipment within or without the plant.

Cooperation with Quality Control in solution of problems connected with production machinery.

Improvement of existing production machinery to improve product or production, reduce maintenance or down time.

Results:

1. Determined cause of rapid wear of German-made dies for punching track in film. Improved die life from 6 weeks to 11 months. As costly dies required 10 to 12 months for delivery, also resulted in substantial savings in inventory.

2. Improved operation of film and paper backing slitting machines entirely eliminating a loss of 3 cuts in every 30, and a second loss of 4 in 12 on second coating of same film, thereby compounding the savings on tens of thousands of film rolls daily.

3. Eliminated costly die purchase by creation of fixture to make deckle edge dies in company shop.

4. Conceived idea of recutting to smaller standard size film which was formerly discarded for improper slitting. Supervised rework of machine (formerly used for different purpose). Savings have exceeded $2,500 monthly.

5. Revamped inoperative machines; accomplished major rejuvenation of production machines.

Reason for desiring change: To be discussed at interview.

REFERENCES

Available

Synopsis of Resume of:
NICHOLAS A. ROCHE

78 Doyle St.
Trenton, NJ 08607
Phone: (609) 242-9003

JOB OBJECTIVE

Position as Traffic Manager or Assistant

EMPLOYMENT

1979-Present	ELECTRONIC DIVISION OF UNITED ELECTROCOM, INC., Trenton, NJ Yearly income has increased by $12,500 since 1979. Senior rate clerk.
1976-1979	ALLIED TRANSPORT COMPANY, Perth Amboy, NJ Assistant Terminal Manager.

EDUCATION

1974	Carver High School, St. Paul, MN

1975	Traffic Managers Institute, Perth Amboy, NJ
	    Course in ICC Law and Procedure.
	Braden Institute, Trenton, NJ. Night School.
	    Course in Traffic Management. Graduated 1st in
	    class.

PERSONAL

Born: 12/5/54. Married, three children; health--good.
Hobbies: Do-it-yourself home projects; spectator sports.
Affiliations: Transportation Club of Trenton.
Civic: Former Vice Pres. of Little Leagues of Perth Amboy, NJ.

(FOR AMPLIFICATION SEE FOLLOWING)

Amplified Resume   Nicholas A. Roche
                                                        -page 2-

                            EMPLOYMENT

1979-Present
ELECTRONIC DIVISION OF UNITED ELECTROCOM, INC.

   1979
   Employed as Junior Rate Clerk; processed and audited freight bills,
   traced shipments. After four months was put in charge of scheduling
   shipments from new warehouse at distance from plant. Ordered and
   scheduled trucks, routed shipments, set up operations which were
   turned over to regular shipping group. Accomplished in less than
   two months.

   1980
   Promoted to Senior Rate Clerk. Actually assumed duties of Traffic
   Manager, as title holder was made Purchasing Agent and spent full
   time in that function. Had complete supervision over personnel,
   gave assignments, made contacts with transportation companies,
   routed shipments, etc. During this period devised routing charts,
   revamped filing system, set up rate charts, leveled distribution so
   equitably among carriers that exceptional shipping service was obtained.

   1982
   On return of aforementioned Traffic Manager to department, was given
   salary raise and unofficial title of Assistant Traffic Manager; formal classification remained Senior Rate Clerk. Handles all technical matters within the department; attends meetings of the Traffic
   and Rate Committee (nationwide). Is familiar with all procedures,
   regulations, laws, and tariffs; does some import and export work.

   Savings: As a result of personal efforts, company has used inter-
      coastal shipping instead of rail. Has shown 40% savings on
      sizable electronic component shipments.

   Reason for desiring change: Position fully utilizing on-the-job
   experience and training as well as recently completed advanced traffic mgmt. course.

1976-1979
ALLIED TRANSPORT CO.

   Employed as manifest clerk; promoted to Rate and Billing Clerk, to
   Office Manager supervising previous work and clerks. Transferred to
   Trenton as Assistant Terminal Manager. Left to accept better
   position above.

                       References Available

Synopsis of Resume of:
ANN MARIE TURNER

4087 Helene St.
Sarasota, FL 33581
Phone: (813) 922-7980

OBJECTIVE

Elementary School Teacher

EMPLOYMENT

1973-Present   SARASOTA COUNTY SCHOOLS, Sarasota, FL
                 Sixth grade teacher

1970-1973   UNIVERSITY OF MIAMI, Miami, FL
                 Laboratory Technician

1964-1970   COMMUNITY CONSOLIDATE SCHOOL DISTRICT, Arlington
                 Hgts., IL
                 Sixth grade science teacher

1960-1962   WHITEHALL CITY SCHOOLS, Columbus, OH
                 Seventh grade teacher

EDUCATION

1974   LaVerne College, LaVerne, CA
         Master's degree in Elementary Education
1960   Ohio State University, Columbus, OH
         B.S. in Education

Other: Ongoing workshops and seminars in science field.

PERSONAL

Born: 1939; single; no children; excellent health; willing to relocate.

Hobbies: Tennis; travel; swimming; needlework; reading.

Affiliations:

Ohio State University Alumni Association; PTA; National Education Association; United Teaching Profession; Sarasota County Teachers Association; Women's Network.

(FOR AMPLIFICATION SEE FOLLOWING)

Technique for consolidating pertinent job experience for present objective.

Amplified Resume   Ann Marie Turner
                                                             -page 2-

TEACHING EXPERIENCE

1973-Present
SARASOTA COUNTY SCHOOLS

1973 - Employed as instructor in an experimental school trying new
       educational concepts. Responsible for mixed classroom of three
       grade levels, planning, teaching, guiding, and evaluating stu-
       dents.

1975 - Voluntary transfer to south country school in Venice, FL. Taught
       approximately 30 students in sixth grade only, in self-contained
       classroom. Subjects: math, language arts (spelling, reading,
       and English), social studies, science.

1982 - When county changed to Middle School concept, eliminating sixth
       grade which was absorbed within the new concept, opted to return
       to Sarasota Brookside School, nearer personal residence.

       Teaches in team situation, consisting of three teachers responsi-
       ble for approximately 90 students. Initially responsible for
       science subjects only; in 1984 language arts were added; pre-
       sently teaches both subjects during a seven-period day.

Reason for desiring change: Has received standard salary raises as
negotiated by Board of Education and Teachers Union; would make change
to area with higher salary scale.

1960-1970
OHIO AND ILLINOIS SCHOOLS

1960 - Employed at Whitehall Schools in first job out of college, as
       teacher of seventh grade; left for marriage and change of resi-
       dence to Illinois.

1964 - Taught sixth grade science at Jr. High level in Arlington,
       Illinois; left to relocate in Florida in 1970.

                         ******

1970-1973
UNIVERSITY OF MIAMI, Miami, FL

Employed as laboratory technician at the Veterans Hospital, working on
a drug research study for United Chemical Co. Duties included: drawing and processing blood; assisting physician in patient examinations;
patient records; correspondence; attendance at autopsies. Left to return to teaching profession.

                      References available

Synopsis of Resume of:
LINDA ROTH

3 Woodthrush Dr.
West Nyack, NY 10994
Phone: (914) 358-7917

JOB OBJECTIVE

Position as social worker with focus on contacts within
therapeutic community

EXPERIENCE

1980-Present   Rockland Community Health Center, Pamona, NY
                    Field Placement

1975-1980   Ontario County Counseling Services, Canandaigua, NY
                    Individual, marital, and family counseling

Prior   Community Service
                    Member two state commissions to oversee
                    Equality of care in state and not-for-profit
                        residential facility

                    Board member and officer in human service agencies
                      for advocacy and services

EDUCATION

College: St. Thomas College, Sparkill, NY
                    B.A. Major - English; minor - Education.

Graduate: Fordham University Graduate School Social Services
                    Degree: M.S.W.
                    Major: services to individuals and families
                    Minor: services to groups.

Other: Certificate in Data Processing.

PERSONAL

Born: 1940; three self-supporting children; excellent health.
Hobbies: Travel; handicrafts; duplicate bridge.
Affiliations: National Association of Social Workers; member Associa-
                    tion for Retarded Children; League of Women Voters.

(FOR AMPLIFICATION SEE FOLLOWING)

Amplified Resume   Linda Roth
                                                         -page 2-

EMPLOYMENT HIGHLIGHTS

1980-Present
ROCKLAND COMMUNITY HEALTH CENTER

Employed as member of crisis intervention team whose responsibilities
include short- and long-term treatment of patients, both adolescents
and adults. Includes full range of diagnostic categories as well as
wide socioeconomic backgrounds.

Given added responsibility of co-therapist in weekly crisis intervention
group handling variety of intra-psychic and personal problems. Includes
emergency suicide and hospitalization evaluation intake and diagnostic
assessment. Periodic consultations with psychiatrists and community
agencies.

Is currently spearheading project to establish spouse and child abuse
center and support team.

Reason for desiring change: Would consider change to less stressful
position within the therapeutic community.

1975-1980
ONTARIO COUNTY COUNSELING SERVICES

Hired on part-time basis, was promoted to full-time status after six
months.

With referrals from family court and probation departments as well as
community agencies, did individual, marital, and family counseling, including intake-diagnostic assessment.

In 1977, was given added responsibility for screening and training new
volunteer counselors, as well as public relations. Addressed community
organizations to increase public awareness of programs and periodic
need for volunteers.

Reason for leaving: To accept better position above.

REFERENCES

On request

Synopsis of Resume of:
ELLIOT N. HALE

159 Antlers Dr.
Duluth, MN 55802
Phone: (218) 643-4962

POSITION OBJECTIVE

Patent Attorney

EXPERIENCE

1980-Present PATENT ATTORNEY (Associate)
Armstron & McKenzie, Patent Attorneys
Duluth, MN

1976-1980 PATENT ATTORNEY
Bigelow Manufacturing Co., Division General Bronze Corp.
Pittsburgh, PA

1975-1976 PATENT ENGINEER
General Electric Co., Washington, D.C.

1970-1975 Private Law Practice
Philadelphia, PA

QUALIFICATIONS

Education: L.L.B. 1969 from Georgetown University, Washington, D.C.
Admitted to Bar, State of Penna. 1970.

Certification: Member Minnesota State Bar. Admission to practice before U.S. Patent Office, U.S. Court of Customs and Patent Appeals, U.S. Court of Claims, U.S. Supreme Court.

PERSONAL

Born: 5/26/45. Married. Health: excellent.
Hobbies: Chess; golf; spectator sports.

(FOR AMPLIFICATION SEE FOLLOWING)

The resume stresses certification and experience to whet employer reading interest. Better than average speaking ability of applicant will sustain employer interest in detail during interview.

Amplified Resume

Elliot N. Hale
-page 2-

EXPERIENCE

1980-Present
ARMSTRON & McKENZIE
Patent Attorneys

    Association with firm to prepare and prosecute patent applications, advise and render opinions on infringement questions and related matters.

    Content with association; however, feels income not in line with responsibilities. Desires industrial connection, preferably in New England area.

1976-1980
BIGELOW MANUFACTURING CO., Division, General Bronze Corp.

    As patent attorney prepared and prosecuted patent applications covering the electrical and electromechanical arts.

    Desired position which required not only preparation and prosecution of patent application, but infringement, licensing, and litigations. Offered and accepted present post which promised added scope.

1975-1976
GENERAL ELECTRIC CO.

    After discussion with head of G.E. Patent Division, was offered and accepted position as Patent Engineer in Washington, D.C. office. Made arrangements to study patent law; was admitted to practice before the U.S. patent office.

    Family situation necessitated return to Pennsylvania area.

1970-1975
PRIVATE PRACTICE

    Upon admission to the bar, set up office with partner in Philadelphia. Engaged in private practice of law which included the following: commercial practice, contract matters, real estate, receiverships, and bankruptcy. Also engaged in the formation of, as well as serving as an officer for, various corporations. In addition, was clerk of Mortgage and Real Estate Committee for the Assembly in the Pennsylvania State Legislature.

    Established excellent reputation; dissolved highly successful partnership to accept offer above which offered opportunity to pursue interest in patent law.

References available

Synopsis of Resume of:
SARAH RYAN

303 Lawton Rd.
Orlando, FL 32803
Phone: (305) 423-5316

JOB OBJECTIVE

Legal Assistant (Paralegal); position in private law firm

EMPLOYMENT

1982-Present	PUBLIC DEFENDER, Orlando, Florida Investigator
1976-1982	SELF-EMPLOYED, Bradenton, Florida. Owned and managed 75-rental-unit complex
1975-1976	FARMERS BANK OF STATE OF DELAWARE, Georgetown, Delaware Supervisor of Mortgage Loan Dept. Moved from area
Prior	ALL AMERICAN ENGINEERING CO., Wilmington, Delaware Assistant to Technical Editor

EDUCATION

1980-1982   Manatee Junior College, Bradenton, Florida (attended nights).
Associate of Science Degree in Legal Assistant Program. 72 hours.

Courses included:

Accounting, Economics, Written Communications, Government, Human Relations, Law Office Management and Procedures, Legal Terminology, Research, Real Property Law, Wills, Trusts and Probate, Principles of Family Law, Civil and Criminal Procedures, General Law, Introduction to Litigation and Evidence, Criminal Law.

PERSONAL

Born: 1/2/44; single; health--excellent; owns home and car.
Hobbies: Spectator sports; sailing; reading.
Affiliations: Member National Association of Legal Assistants, Inc.
Member Orlando Sailing Club.

(FOR AMPLIFICATION SEE FOLLOWING)

Woman who decided to change fields and pursue a lifelong interest in law. "Talked herself" into a good job in this comparatively new field. Resume focus strictly on legal aspect.

Amplified Resume   Sarah Ryan
                                                           -page 2-

LEGAL EMPLOYMENT HIGHLIGHTS

1982 - Present

> After receiving Associate Degree as Legal Assistant, approached
> Public Defender requesting permission to work as intern for a three-
> month period at no salary in order to gain additional practical, on-
> the-job experience and training. Request granted.
>
> At conclusion of trial period was offered and accepted full-time
> position of "Investigator."
>
> In this capacity, primary function is handling Juvenile and Misde-
> meanor investigations, as well as overflow of felony cases.
>
> Interviews incarcerated defendants and assists them in obtaining
> reasonable bonds. Interviews persons being held in Juvenile Deten-
> tion for daily hearings.
>
> Assists "walk-ins" needing help and advice on a court proceeding as
> well as general information pertaining to the processes involved in
> obtaining a public defender (prior to arraignment).
>
> Does follow-up work relative to interviews; interviews witnesses,
> arranges for photographs, makes all diagrams and tabulates any rela-
> ted evidence for use in ultimate defense. Evaluates, coordinates
> all evidence and information, which is discussed with attorneys.
>
> Maintains good public relations with all other governmental agencies
> involved in the Criminal Justice System, as well as the lawyers and
> co-workers in Public Defender's employ.
>
> Attends professional seminars to keep abreast of new methods, pro-
> cedures, and general updating to aid and improve job performance.
>
> Reason for desiring change: Thoroughly enjoys work and responsibili-
> ties; would make change only to private law firm with greater
> remuneration and less pressure.

REFERENCES

Available. Please do not contact present employer at this time.

Synopsis of Resume of: 890 Maple Ave.
AUDREY BRANDT   Irvine, CA 92714
                                          Phone: (714) 334-8973

OBJECTIVE

Travel Agent/Consultant

EXPERIENCE

1982-1985   WORLEY TRAVEL AGENCY, Los Angeles, CA
                     Travel Consultant

1975-1982   LOS ANGELES COUNTY, Los Angeles, CA
                     Social Worker

1974-1975   Personal travel: Africa, China, Mexico

EDUCATION

1970-1975   Bennington College, Port Washington, NY
                     B.A. degree; major - psychology.

1981-1982   Los Angeles City College
                     Travel Agent Course (nights)

Current: Institute of Certified Travel Agents
                     Enrolled in "Certified Travel Counselor" course
                 given on seminar basis. Covers business, personnel,
                 marketing, and travel. Geared toward pursuit of ex-
                 cellence and professionalism in the travel field.

PERSONAL

Age: 31   Single; excellent health; free to relocate.
Hobbies: Raising Shelties; gardening; latch hooking.
Affiliations: Junior League; member Individual Travel Agents.

(FOR AMPLIFICATION SEE FOLLOWING)

Amplified Resume

Audrey Brandt
-page 2-

EXPERIENCE

1982-1985
WORLEY TRAVEL AGENCY

Employed as trainee; in six months promoted to full-time "travel consultant" in this eight-employee agency which caters to an affluent, knowledgeable clientele.

Consulted and advised clients in trip planning; made computerized airline reservations; phoned for land, rail, hotel, and car reservations. Collected payments; paid suppliers; followed up on final documents and details, as well as problems and complaints.

Made periodic, expense-paid trips to check out hotel, ship, and accommodations in general, in advance of recommendation to clients.

Destinations have included: Spain, Russia, Alaska, and the Caribbean Islands.

Reason for leaving: To be discussed at interview.

1975-1982
LOS ANGELES COUNTY

Employed as social worker in the "Aid to the Disabled" branch of this very large agency.

Interviewed over 300 families per year, computing their welfare budgets based on need.

Promoted to assistant medical social worker working with the elderly and disabled.

Resigned to move into more upbeat travel field.

REFERENCES

On request

Synopsis of Resume of
WENDY WAINWRIGHT

307 Copperwood Ct.
Colleyville, TX 76034
Phone: (817) 987-5602

OBJECTIVE

Airline Flight Attendant

EMPLOYMENT

1981-1985   SOUTHERN AIRLINES, Miami, FL
From reservations agent to flight attendant.
Left for marriage and relocation out-of-state.

Prior   GIRL SCOUTS OF AMERICA
Water Safety Instructor, Waterfront Director,
summers during high school and college.

EDUCATION

1978-1980   Katharine Gibbs School, New York, City
Secretarial and business courses, with
emphasis on grooming, poise, presence.

Skills: Typing; computer knowledge; fluent Spanish,
working knowledge of French.

PERSONAL

Age: 24   Single; height: 5'7"; weight: 125; excellent health.
Hobbies: Aerobics; swimming; classical music.

(FOR AMPLIFICATION SEE FOLLOWING)

Note: To slant resume to a specific airline, call the local office and ask for address to write for brochure listing qualifications, and application blank. Major airlines are cooperative and happy to oblige with information on all available positions and requirements.

Among positions at airlines other than flight attendants: Customer Service Agent; Clerk-Typist; General Clerical; Reservations Sales Agent; Customer Service Support Agent; Maintenance Utility Employee.

Amplified Resume

EXPERIENCE

1981-1985
SOUTHERN AIRLINES

Employed immediately following college as reservations sales agent assigned to the Miami, FL office.

Given orientation and training in sophisticated computers, as well as telephone sales training in convincing prospective customers telephoning for flight information of merits of airline.

Upon reaching age 20, made application and was selected for four-week Flight Attendant training program. Covered every aspect of responsibilities:

>   Technical and operational instruction; customer service orientation; safety; security; emergency procedures; infant care; swift food/beverage service procedures; personal grooming; poise.

Assigned to Flight Attendant base station in Miami, flew approximately 70 hours each month. Excellent record of attendance and fulfillment of assigned duties; given performance rating of "Above Average," plus periodic salary raises.

Reason for leaving:

Left for marriage and relocation out-of-state. Currently eager to resume career as Flight Attendant. Free to relocate anywhere in the United States.

REFERENCES

On request

Part 3

For Women Returning To The Job Market

DISPLACED HOMEMAKERS

Not too many years ago, when a woman who was "just a housewife" was widowed, divorced, or separated, she was left alone to fend for herself. Now, such a woman has been raised to the status of "Displaced Homemaker" and is receiving support services from local Displaced Homemaker Re-Entry Programs.

According to a co-founder of the Displaced Homemaker Movement, there are an estimated 189,000 displaced homemakers in New England alone. This indicates a national figure that is quite substantial.

The official definition of a displaced homemaker is a person (usually over age thirty-five) who has worked in the home providing unpaid services for a family for a number of years, and is forced suddenly into the labor market.

Although the removal of age discrimination barriers is a pragmatic solution to the older person's job hunt, it's realistic to acknowledge that certain psychological barriers remain. It's up to the erstwhile "housewife" to hammer away at the image until it is changed, and it's gradually happening. The motivation is sheer survival—and it's a strong one.

Look for a Displaced Homemakers Program in your area. If none is available, call local high schools for adult education course listings. They often include peer group rap sessions with titles such as "Widow to Widow Lift" or "Divorce, A New Beginning."

An alternative is to take a refresher course in an old skill: typing, bookkeeping, sewing, home decorating, cake decorating, flower arranging, creative writing.

Make use of your transferable skills. Restaurants use good cooking and baking skills. Florists use flower arranging skills. Stores use salespersons knowledgeable about children's clothing, housewares, and home decorating.

Displaced homemakers may need their confidence bolstered. A volunteer job is a good start. It provides needed structure in grooming, being someplace on time at definite hours, and mixing with strangers, and increases a sense of self-worth.

The paying job for the displaced homemaker reentering the labor market is often at the entry level, a fact of life acknowledged by the Labor Department. However, the sky's the limit once she's in, and a proper resume can immeasurably aid the entry.

This section of the book contains sample resumes of displaced homemakers with various degrees of skills and experience, as well as varied goals.

Synopsis of Resume of: 9876 Venice Blvd.
MARILYN NEAL CULLEN   Culver City, CA 90034
                                               Phone: (213) 352-9007

OBJECTIVE

Position with potential requiring good verbal and writing skills;
 advertising, copywriting. Would consider sales with potential.

EXPERIENCE

1984-Present   SALES
                 Mail order sportswear sold through party plan.

1975-1984   FREELANCE WRITING
                 Part-time while raising family.

1974   DRESS SHOP MANAGER
                 "Mary Del Shop" women's apparel.

Prior   Before marriage was Assistant Fashion Coordinator,
                 and Assistant to Advertising Director for shoe company.

EDUCATION

College: Nassau Community College, Garden City, NY
                    Major: English Literature

Other: Betty Owen Secretarial Systems
                    Shorthand 100 WPM; Typing 60 WPM
                 George Mercer School of Theology
                    Degree in Religious Education

PERSONAL

Age: Mature, four children, two self-supporting.
Health: Good.
Hobbies: Music; sewing; sketching; writing.
Affiliations: Member, church choir; Literary Club.

(FOR AMPLIFICATION SEE FOLLOWING)

Sales picked from record to focus on qualifications for objective.

Amplified Resume   Marilyn Neal Cullen
                                                    -page 2-

EXPERIENCE HIGHLIGHTS

1984-Present
SALES

   Interim work while seeking full-time career objective. Sells line
   of women's sportswear through home party plan. Makes own contacts,
   sets up appointments, models and shows line. Takes orders and follows through to delivery and customer satisfaction. Increased sales
   to point where has hired an assistant.

1975-1984
FREELANCE WRITING

   During years of marriage and raising family worked from home doing
   freelance writing assignments. Included writing and editing travel
   guide for "Association of Informed Travelers," a series of articles
   on an experimental educational project, and radio copy.

   During this period did church-related volunteer work. Appointed
   Prayer Chairman responsible for opening and closing board meetings
   as well as luncheon invocations, was promoted to General Chairman.
   In this capacity multiple functions included: chairing 20-member
   board meetings, coordinating public luncheon meetings for up to 140
   persons.

1974
MANAGEMENT

   As Manager for women's apparel shop, "Mary Del," hired and supervised sales personnel, scheduled floor time, and assisted in closing
   sales. Did all bookkeeping and banking. Left because of pregnancy.

Prior

   Following college, employed by Chas. Stevens Co. of St. Louis in
   Lingerie Dept. Promoted to manager of department, supervised full
   and part-time employees, gained experience in all aspects, including
   inventory.

   Filled in as model for in-store fashion shows, given additional responsibility as Assistant Fashion Coordinator. Named member of
   "Shoe Fashion Board of St. Louis," one of five women who met monthly
   formulating articles and giving interviews to local news media on
   fashion trends in shoe industry. Designed and modeled shoes; acted
   as liaison between factory and store. Left for marriage.

REFERENCES

Available

Synopsis of Resume of: 875 Sparkman Blvd.
ELEANOR OWEN   Tucson, AZ 85716
                                                Phone: (602) 884-9633

JOB OBJECTIVE

Executive Director, preferably with non-profit organization

EXPERIENCE

1982-Present   SENIOR FRIENDSHIP CENTER, Tucson, AZ
                    Director

1980-1982   HOME CARE CORPS FOR SENIOR CITIZENS, Pittsburgh, PA.
                    Supervisor

1976-1980   COMMUNITY ADVOCATE, JOB DEVELOPER, Boston, MA
                    Boston, MA

1966-1976   CHARLES STONE ASSOCIATES, Boston, MA
                    Economist

Prior: NYS DEPT. OF LABOR, Rome, NY
                    Labor Market Analyst

                CHAMBER OF COMMERCE, Oak Ridge, TN
                    Manager

                Public School Teacher

EDUCATION

B.A.   Boston University - Economics, Business Administration

M.S.   Brooklyn College - Economic Development and Education

Other: Special courses in: Administration of Voluntary Civic
            Organizations; Job Analysis; Administration and Planning
            of Social Service Delivery Programs; Evaluation of Social
            Security Development Programs; Supervision in a Social
            Service Agency.

PERSONAL

Mature, in good health, owns and drives car, free to travel or relocate.

(FOR AMPLIFICATION SEE FOLLOWING)

Amplified Resume

Eleanor Owen
-page 3-

EXPERIENCE

1982-Present
SENIOR FRIENDSHIP CENTER

Director of state-funded program. Plans and supervises program, including training, counseling, liaison with community resources, outreach, and public relations. Feels degree of authority assured has been fragmented; would make change for similar position with full reign.

1980-1982
HOME CARE CORPS FOR SENIOR CITIZENS

Supervised staff of 30. Directed eight programs funded under Title III of the Older Americans Act, including Shuttle Service, Income Maintenance, Housing Advocacy, and Visiting Aides. Planned, supervised housing outreach program. Interviewed 78% of the target population; supervised preparation of submitted report. Left for new challenge above.

1976-1980
COMMUNITY ADVOCATE

Headed up project "Retain." Responsibilities included outreach, public relations, volunteer supervision, intake interviews, job placement and development. Goal: to change attitude of business community toward the employment of the older job seeker in private industry. Project satisfactorily completed.

1966-1976
CHARLES STONE ASSOCIATES

Researched and developed criteria for public facilities grants to localities to alleviate long-term unemployment. Wrote proposals on cost/benefit criteria for "Safety on the Highway" grants.

NYS DEPT. OF LABOR

Employed on special project as labor market analyst to explore employment status of displaced Sperry Rand employees several months after company moved to another area. Results showed direct correlation between the employee's age and present employment status.

CHAMBER OF COMMERCE

Supervised budget, community relations, membership drives and chamber's multiple committees. Planned and wrote an economic analysis of region. Organized Tourist Bureau. Increased membership by 20%, tourist inquiries by 50%.

References on request

Synopsis of Resume of: 29 South St.
REGINA T. BRODY   Minneapolis, MN 55401
                                               Phone: (612) 333-1989

JOB OBJECTIVE

Editing, Writing, Research. Free to travel on own or as assistant.

EMPLOYMENT

Present   RESEARCH ASSISTANT
                 Assistant to author of book on American Art Museums.
                 Part-time work on hourly pay scale.

1974-1984   VOLUNTEER WORK.
                 Director Parent-Child Day Care Center.
                 Teacher's aide and tutor in public schools.

Prior   DEMONSTRATION SCHOOL OF NATIONAL COLLEGE OF EDUCATION
                 Teacher

                 WIEBOLDT FOUNDATION FUNDED PROJECT
                 Science Consultant and Assistant

EDUCATION

B.A. Wellesley College, Wellesley, MA
M.Ed. National College of Education, Evanston, IL

PUBLICATIONS

Young People's Science Encyclopedia - Science Editor.
Science Activities From A to Z - co-author.
Value Sharing: Creative Strategy - co-author.

PERSONAL

Age: Mature, recent widow; three self-supporting children.
Health: Excellent.
Hobbies: Tennis; golf; travel; theater; music.
Affiliations: Wellesley Club; American Pen Women's Club.

(FOR AMPLIFICATION SEE FOLLOWING)

*Analysis: Well-educated woman. Has substantial private income, subtly indicated by
job objective, and expertise to back up goal documented by listed "publications."*

Amplified Resume

Regina T. Brody
- page 2-

EXPERIENCE HIGHLIGHTS

Present
RESEARCH ASSISTANT

Recommended by local art gallery to an author who is researching book on American Museums. Edited his work, as well as doing additional research on own; has written short biographical sketches of selected artists. Project scheduled for completion late this year. Hourly wage doubled since work began; excellent letter of reference available.

1974-1984
VOLUNTEER WORK

Wife of successful banker and in no need of income, became actively engaged in community projects on volunteer basis. Assisted in fundraising drive to establish a Parent-Child Day Care Center, and served as its director for four years. Full-time five-day-week responsibilities. Acted as teacher's aide and science tutor at both junior high and elementary public school level.

Prior
DEMONSTRATION SCHOOL OF NATIONAL COLLEGE OF EDUCATION

In addition to teaching sixth grade, was responsible for supervision of student teachers. Did demonstration lessons for closed-circuit television, lecturing to students enrolled in the various college courses. Required careful course preparation as well as interesting presentation to sustain viewer interest. Supervised student participation in the program. Resigned when husband was transferred from area.

RESEARCH PROJECT

Employed as Science Consultant and Assistant to administrator of research project funded by Wieboldt Foundation in Chicago. Project structured around a social-psychological framework developed by Harold Lasswell of Yale. Staffed by National College of Education and administered in five Chicago schools (K through 8). Edited final report.

REFERENCES

On request. Copies of publications available for review.

Synopsis of Resume of: 59 E. Connor St.
JANET PIERCE   Sheridan, WY 82801
                                               Phone: (307) 324-4760

JOB OBJECTIVE

Freelance writing

EDUCATION

College   Milwaukee-Downer College, Milwaukee, Wisconsin
                 B.A. Major: English Literature

                 University of Michigan
                 Graduate work, teacher's certificate courses.

                 Findlay College, Findlay, Ohio.
                 Business courses. Typing, shorthand, dictaphone.

                 Columbia University.
                 Journalism Workshop.

Other: Languages.
                 Fluent Spanish; working knowledge of French.

EMPLOYMENT

1982-Present   Shopping Guide, Inc., Sheridan, Wyoming.
                 Food columnist.

Prior   Oakland Press, Pontiac, Michigan.
                 Women's Editor. Promoted from part-time food writer.

                 Pontiac Michigan Board of Education.
                 Taught speech and creative writing adult education
                 classes

PERSONAL

Age: Mature; married; excellent health.
Hobbies: Reading; jogging; cooking; crafts; theater; music.
Affiliations: Member: AAUW, National Federation of Press Women.
                 Board member of Friends of Arts and Sciences and com-
                 munity theater group.

(FOR AMPLIFICATION SEE FOLLOWING)

*Mature woman endowed with high energy as indicated by eagerness to take
continued education courses and remain involved with or without pay.*

Amplified Resume   Janet Pierce
                                                           -page 2-

EMPLOYMENT HIGHLIGHTS

1982-Present
SHOPPING GUIDE, INC. (weekly newspaper)

Following husband's retirement to Wyoming, approached paper with
idea of writing a food column featuring various items advertised
as "weekly specials" by food markets. Given trial period at no
salary; however, idea proved so successful was hired as weekly
columnist and given bonus for increased food advertising, which
has resulted.

Reason for change: Required to be in newspaper office several days
a week. Would like position working out of own home.

PRIOR

Oakland Press, Pontiac, Michigan.

Employed as part-time food writer. Steadily advanced to Food Editor,
Home Editor, and Feature Writer. During tenure gained thorough
knowledge of all newspaper aspects, including importance of meeting
deadlines, dependability, and professionalism.

Was promoted to Women's Editor, while continuing as Food Editor.
Job terminated with sale of newspaper to Tri-Cities, which brought
in own staff.

Pontiac Board of Education

Simultaneous with above, volunteered to teach creative writing and
speech classes for evening adult education classes. Three students
moved on to successful, professional writing careers.

Girl Scouts of America

Filled in for Girl Scout Executive during six-month temporary leave
of absence. Is skilled in, and taught variety of crafts.

REFERENCES

On request

Synopsis of Resume of: 9778 Hickman Rd.
LORETTA WILKINSON   Des Moines, IA 50322
                                                Phone: (515) 281-8596

JOB OBJECTIVE

Medical field combined with general office. Job interest more
                    important than salary.

EDUCATION

Drake University, Des Moines, IA
     Liberal Arts

Pine Shores Hospital, Kansas City, MO
     Completed Ward Clerk Course. 435 hours.

Skills: Typing, speedwriting, adding machine, calculator.
                Familiarity with medical terminology.

CAREER EXPERIENCE

1970-1975   INTERNAL REVENUE SERVICE, Kansas City, MO
                     Secretary to Chief

Prior   IOWA-DES MOINES NATIONAL BANK, Des Moines, IA
                     Secretary to Vice-President

                GENERAL HOSPITAL, Des Moines, IA
                     Volunteer hospital work in varied capacities

PERSONAL

Born: Mature; widow; excellent health.
Finances: Good order; owns home, car, income property.
Hobbies: Tennis; crossword puzzles; genealogy research.
Affiliations: St. Andrews Society; Brentwood Country Club.

(FOR AMPLIFICATION SEE FOLLOWING)

*Financially independent "displaced homemaker" who has been gainfully employed in
earlier years and wishes to reenter job market in other than volunteer capacity,
conveyed by objective's "job interest." No-date "career highlights" point up
capabilities while soft-pedaling homemaking years.*

Amplified Resume   Loretta Wilkinson
                                                          -page 2-

CAREER CHRONOLOGY

Iowa-Des Moines National Bank

Immediately following college, employed as secretary to vice-president. Performed standard secretarial functions: dictation, typing, bookkeeping, and filing, utilizing and honing basic skills acquired during part-time stenographic jobs during high school. Left for marriage.

Internal Revenue Service, Kansas City, Missouri

With family raised, took job as secretary to Chief, Field Audit for the State of Missouri. Took dictation, typed letters, received visitors, received and sorted mail. Kept time and attendance reports for 100 personnel, as well as statutory period of limitation control cards. Left because of husband's illness and returned to Des Moines.

Transcon Industries

Working out of home, became local distributor for Transcon Industries. Bought the costume jewelry ring distributorship, serviced boutiques, beauty shops, drug stores, and dress shops. Succeeded in establishing 25 lucrative accounts before company went out of business.

Miscellaneous

Volunteer work in hospitals and Ward Clerk course afforded experience and knowledge in:
    Maintaining patient charts and records.
    Transcribing doctors' orders for medical records.
    Programming patient medications, tests, and diets.
    Ordering supplies, blood, and drugs from hospital pharmacist.
    Graphing vital statistics for nurses; receiving patients.
    Maintaining costs incurred for patient treatment.

REFERENCES

On request

Synopsis of Resume of: 490 Palomino Rd.
AGNES MORROW   Phoenix, AZ 85013
                                          Phone: (602) 433-9872

JOB OBJECTIVE

Newspaper Field: writing, editing, features

EXPERIENCE

1980-Present   Interim position as sales representative for
                financial group of luxury condominium. Primary
                function: writing sales letters, advertising copy,
                and in-house organization. Would like to resume
                newspaper career.

1967-1980   Homemaker

1966-1967   WORLD JOURNAL TRIBUNE, New York City
                    Rewrite and Feature Writer

1955-1966   WORLD TELEGRAM AND SUN, New York City
                    Assistant Editor - Feature/Columnist

1953-1955   BROOKLYN EAGLE, Brooklyn, NY
                    General Assignment Reporter

1951-1953   SAN ANTONIO EXPRESS AND EVENING NEWS, TX
                    Photojournalist

EDUCATION

1948-1951   Syracuse University, Syracuse, NY
                    B.A. - major, Journalism; minor - Business Ad-
                    ministration

PERSONAL

Born: 1922; widow, two grown children, self-supporting;
                free to relocate.
Hobbies: swimming, boating; reading; sewing.

Affiliations

Former member: Newspaper Women's Club of New York; Newspaper Reporters'
Association; Society of the Silurians (members elected from those who
have worked 15 or more years on a NYC newspaper); Theta Sigma Phi
(women's journalism honorary society).

(FOR AMPLIFICATION SEE FOLLOWING)

*Resume technique for "displaced homemaker" who wants to reenter field in which
she has impressive record.*

Amplified Resume   Agnes Morrow
                                                        -page 2-

NEWSPAPER CAREER HIGHLIGHTS

1951-1963
San Antonio Express

During two-year tenure was assigned to magazine staff doing feature-
writing and expected to take own pictures. Improved steadily as photographer under coaching of staff photographer. Worked closely with art
staff in layout; learned nuts and bolts of newspaper business including
writing picture captions and heads. Resigned to try larger market in
New York City.

1953-1955
Brooklyn Eagle

In a matter of weeks found job with the Brooklyn Eagle as general
assignment reporter, easily handling faster pace of meeting deadlines
and mixed assignments.

1955-1966
World Telegram and Sun

Upward career move to larger paper, with increase in salary and responsibilities. Promoted to Assistant Editor of the Brooklyn Section,
supervising reportorial staff of ten.

Covered City Hall beat, plus Manhattan and Federal Court. Wrote under
personal by-line, covering wide range of subjects from politics from a
woman's point of view, to art critiques and humor pieces.

1966-1967
World Journal Tribune

Above "World Telegram" merged with two other New York City newspapers
in 1966, to become "World Journal Tribune." Worked as feature writer
and spot news, as well as rewrite for the City Desk. Full responsibility for the Sunday edition.

Reason for Leaving:

Left newspaper field after marriage in 1967, to relocate in Arizona
where husband's employment was centered.

REFERENCES

Newspapers listed above are now defunct. Has portfolio of by-line features and articles available for review. Personal references on
request.

NETWORKING

For as long as anyone can remember, the strength and power of "the good old boys," "the men at the club," "the fellows in the lodge," "the guys at lunch," have sustained men in every endeavor.

Professional women today are a new breed. Their needs are many, their aspirations steadily growing. They need a "good old girl" network.

The theory of women's networking is simple. What has worked for men over the years can not only work for women, but can be improved on and flourish. Women helping women—networking, communicating, supporting one another, exchanging information on job concerns, job openings, salary scales, employer preferences, idiosyncrasies. Who's the sweetheart? Who's the brute? Which firms have good benefits? Poor-benefit firms? Dead-end avenues as opposed to those with bright potential?

Women's network chapters are mushrooming all over the country. Their philosophy: "What can I do for you?—What can you do for me?" Look in your local telephone directories to determine if there is one in your area. Call your local Chamber of Commerce or Heads-Up business women's organizations if there are none listed.

Most women's networks meet monthly, and have an official directory of members listed along with profession categories. Meetings are informal, chatty, constructive, and fun. There are no dues, no obligations; you've nothing to lose and much to gain.

Organizations to write to for referrals for networking groups are:

Displaced Homemakers Network, National Headquarters, 1010 Vermont Avenue, N.W., Suite 817, Washington, D.C. 20005

Catalyst National Headquarters, 14 East 60th Street, New York, N.Y. 10022.

APPENDIX: SENIOR COMMUNITY SERVICE EMPLOYMENT PROGRAM

The Senior Community Service Employment Program (SCSEP) is an employment service that pays you for on-the-job training in community service agencies while helping you find a job with private or public employers.

Sponsored by the American Association of Retired Persons, the Senior Community Service Employment Program is a federally funded employment program designed to assist the older worker (fifty-five or older) in reentering the job market. It operates under a grant from the U.S. Department of Labor under Title V of the Older Americans Act, and clients must have an income which does not exceed the guidelines of the program. Current ceilings are $4,900 for one person, $6,720 for a family of two.

Program enrollees are the employees of AARP and SCSEP and are assigned work in a temporary position at one of a variety of host agencies (community service organizations, non-profit or government agencies, etc.). A client works approximately twenty hours per week and receives no less than the current federal minimum wage or the state minimum wage, whichever is higher.

The goal of the program is to help those enrolled develop job skills and capabilities and to obtain permanent jobs either with the assigned host agency or in the private sector.

Benefits: annual physical examination; sick leave; holidays; worker's compensation insurance; one-year free membership in AARP.

Senior Community Service Employment Programs are active in the locations listed on the following page.

Arkansas
Hot Springs
Little Rock

California
Eureka
Richmond
Sacramento
Santa Cruz
Santa Maria
Santa Rosa
Visalia

Colorado
Colorado Springs

Florida
Clearwater
Dade County
Fort Lauderdale
Gainesville
Jacksonville
Miami
Naples
New Port Richey
Orlando
Pensacola
Pinellas County
Sarasota
St. Petersburg
Tallahassee
Tampa

Georgia
Athens
Atlanta
Augusta
Columbus
Milledgeville
Savannah
Tifton

Idaho
Boise

Illinois
Edwardsville
Peoria
Springfield

Indiana
Indianapolis
Terre Haute

Iowa
Des Moines
Ottumwa
Waterloo

Kentucky
Louisville
Owensboro

Louisiana
New Orleans
Shreveport

Maine
Portland

Massachusetts
Salem

Michigan
Benton Harbor
Escanaba
Grand Rapids
Southgate

Missouri
Kansas City
Springfield
St. Louis

Montana
Billings

Nebraska
Lincoln

Nevada
Clark County
Ely
Sparks

New Hampshire
North Conway

New Mexico
Albuquerque

New York
Bay Shore
Mt. Morris
Poughkeepsie
Riverhead
Utica
Watkins Glen

North Dakota
Fargo

Ohio
Cincinnati
Cleveland
Columbus
Portsmouth
St. Clairsville
Steubenville

Oklahoma
Oklahoma City
Tulsa

Oregon
Portland
Salem

Pennsylvania
Bethlehem
Harrisburg
Johnstown

Puerto Rico
Arecibo
Humacao
Ponce
San Juan

Rhode Island
North Kingstown
Providence

South Carolina
Florence
Greenville

South Dakota
Sioux Falls

Texas
Dallas
Del Rio
Edinburg
El Paso
Harris County
Houston
Laredo
Lubbock
Waco

Virginia
Norfolk
Richmond

Washington
Bellingham
King County
Seattle
Spokane
Wenatchee

Wyoming
Sheridan

For more information write to:

American Association of Retired Persons (AARP), 1909 K Street, N.W., Washington, D.C. 20049.

ARCO BOOKS FOR JOB HUNTERS

RESUMES AND JOB-FINDING GUIDES

How to Get a Job Overseas, *Casewit*

Make Your Job Interview a Success, *Biegeleisen*

Resumes for Better Jobs, *Brennan, Strand, Gruber*

Resumes for Secretaries, *Corwen*

Resumes That Get Jobs, *Resume Service*

The 40+ Job Hunting Guide, *Birsner*

Your Resume: Key to a Better Job, *Corwen*

SKILLS REVIEWS

Arithmetic Simplified and Self-Taught

Bookkeeping Simplified and Self-Taught, *Gorham*

Business English Simplified and Self-Taught, *Brossman*

Business Letters Simplified and Self-Taught, *Farber*

Business Mathematics Simplified and Self-Taught, *Chernon*

Consumer and Business Mathematics, *Meyer*

Mastering Multiple-Choice Mathematics Tests, *Smith*

Mathematics Simplified and Self-Taught, *Erdsneker*

Mechanical Aptitude and Spatial Relations Tests, *Arco Editorial Board*

Scoring High on Analogy Tests, *Steinberg*

Secretary's Quick Reference Handbook, *Lindsell*

Triple Your Typing Speed, *Cutler*

Typing for Everyone, *Levine*

Vocabulary Builder and Verbal Aptitude Test Guide, *Miller, Morse-Cluley*

Webster's New World Guide to Scoring High on Vocabulary Tests, *Morse-Cluley*

ORDER THE BOOKS DESCRIBED IN THE PRECEDING LISTING FROM YOUR BOOKSELLER OR DIRECTLY FROM:

Simon & Schuster Mail Order Billing
Route 59 at Brook Hill Drive
West Nyack, New York 10994

MAIL THIS COUPON TODAY!

Simon & Schuster Mail Order Billing, Route 59 at Brook Hill Drive, West Nyack, NY 10994.
Please rush the following Arco books:

NO. OF COPIES	TITLE #	TITLE	PRICE	EXTENSION
			SUB-TOTAL	
			LOCAL TAX	
		12% PACKING & MAILING		
			TOTAL	

I enclose check ☐, M.O. ☐, for $_____ or charge my ☐ VISA ☐ MASTERCARD

Account #_____ Exp. Date_____

Signature_____

NAME _____

ADDRESS _____

CITY _____ **STATE** _____ **ZIP** _____

*Every Arco book is guaranteed. Return for full refund within ten days
if not completely satisfied.*

NOT RESPONSIBLE FOR CASH SENT THROUGH THE MAILS